Smooth: Tales of a Non-Convicted Criminal, Part II

Smooth, Volume 2

Noel Dias

Published by Noel Dias, 2024.

This is a work of fiction. Similarities to real people, places, or events are entirely coincidental.

SMOOTH: TALES OF A NON-CONVICTED CRIMINAL, PART II

First edition. February 14, 2024.

Written by Noel Dias.

Table of Contents

I dedicate this book to a dear fallen childhood friend, Donnie Ray "Doty Mite" Williams, and Arthur "Youngblood" Carter, who was taken too early by this powerful disease called cancer.

Youngblood would always tell me I was like an educated gangster. He was the one who would listen to my stories through the years and learn about the different schools I attended. I admit that without the passing of my dear friend, this book, or any of my books for that matter, would have never been written because he would still be visiting me every Saturday, making it nearly impossible for me to write. REST, my brother

Disclaimer

This is a book of fiction derived from a nonfictional story. The story is based on actual events that happened in real life, with the storylines being removed from their original sites and the depictions being a mixture of truth and fiction. This story is for entertainment purposes and is not to be taken as anything more. As the book contains a substantial amount of truth, the storylines have been altered with fictional details from the writer's imagination. The characters' names have been changed to protect their innocence. No character's name is used without his or her consent or the consent of a family member. Any provocative sexual scenes have been censored or totally omitted for the safeguarding and decency of the characters at the discretion of the writer. The timeframe and places of the actual events are also strictly from the writer's imagination or are publicly documented establishments that were actually visited

Acknowledgments

First and foremost, I would continue to thank my mother for giving me the spiritual leadership and guidance to believe and trust in God, our Lord and Savior Jesus Christ. I will always remember the last words I heard from my mother before her passing: "Baby, I am so proud of the way you turned out."

I also give thanks to two prominent families I crossed paths within the aftermath of that "It" my mind, body, and soul had to deal with during my early life's journey. They have given me true love with an opportunity to continue life in a respectful way, without any legal interruptions. I can honestly say God could not have put me in the arms of better families for the final stages of this life's journey. They should be acknowledged, even if by nothing more than their initials. Thanks to Mr. D. C. and Mr. J. A., respectfully.

I would like to thank my children, whom I barely know. I'm so proud of how intelligent and successful you've all turned out. I have a chance now to watch my grandchildren perform as they grow up, and I must say, I'm a proud G-daddy. With the hope and prayer that this "It" or "Curse" or whatever was over me shall never return to anyone in our family again.

I can't help but acknowledge the women who had to put up with my horrible and malicious acts while on this tragic assignment. I apologize. I must say once again, if there are any hard feelings you are not able to let go of, I continue to pray for God to give you the strength to do so. And please forgive me, as that person was not the real me. To the character Natalie: you'll know who you are. For all I put you through, again, I apologize.

To Write My Wrongs and its staff, with all pleasure, thanks for allowing me to be a part of something so wonderful. And to my editor, Nate B., without you, this would still be just an idea.

Last but not least, I would like to give a special shout-out to my attorney, whom I had not spoken with in almost forty years until he received a copy of my first "Book." Thank you "JLM" for accepting the opportunity given to both of us. God allowed us to learn from each other during such a misunderstood trial. Over the years, I've cherished every minute I've been given to realize what we shared together. I also appreciate the compliment given to me during our conversation after thirty-nine years. Coming from someone with such great stature, I accept it with honor. I thank you again for believing in me and for keeping my feet planted on God's free soil.

Chapter 1. Meeting the Family

Other than him reminding me from time to time that my narrow escape from the cops was still swirling around in his head, the trip to New York with Moke in the Monte Carlo had been uneventful. The car itself drew attraction. Every time we stopped for gas, people would stand and admire the black-on-black Monte Carlo sitting on a set of three-and-a-half-inch gangster whitewall tires, coupled with a set of chrome Truespoke wheels. The car also sported a luxurious black padded vinyl top and a sunroof.

Moke wasn't much of a conversationalist while riding, but every once in a while, he would make sure that I was still alert and ask if I needed a break. A couple of times I drifted off to sleep only to be awakened by his irritating snores or the rumbling strips on the shoulder of the road. Still, the anticipation of seeing my son who was living with his mother, Karol, in New York melded with the soulful sounds of Earth, Wind & Fire, the Commodores, and of course the Temptations, all of which played on my brand-new in-dash Pioneer cassette player, kept my adrenaline flowing.

As we were traveling through the state of South Carolina, something in the air must have awoken him.

"Vincent, could we stop in Spartanburg? I'd like you to meet my parents."

"Sure! We're not that far away."

He hadn't spoken much about his childhood or his parents, but I loved the idea of meeting them. Whatever it was that awakened him must have come with a thought, as he mentioned spending a few weeks with them.

"Vincent, I must say, you'll have to look over my father. He may be a little different. Some say he's intimidating, and others may say dangerous at times, but in the end, he's a great dad. My mother, on the other hand, is a little old-fashioned but a very generous and warm-hearted person. Humm!"

"What are you humming for?" I asked.

"Just a thought I had."

"Well, you've got me wondering. Could you share that thought?"

"Yeah," he said with a slight frown. "It looks like the lower end of Pine Street has begun to change."

Then he went on to inform me that he could tell something wasn't right. It seemed to me his anxiety started to rise a bit as we continued to drive into the city.

"Take the next left. You can park on the shoulder to the right." He nearly stepped out of the car before it had come to a complete stop. I straggled behind as we walked over a beautiful little arched bridge that crossed over the ditch in front of their house.

He quickly turned and asked, "Vincent, did you lock the doors? You have a habit of not doing so." That sparked me into thinking, all the money I had was in that car stuffed inside my pouch, eight grand to be exact. Heck, I couldn't afford to let someone walk away with it.

"Wait here Moke, I'll be right back." I trotted across the pretty little arched bridge once more to secure the doors. The house stood not far off and had an amazing design that would capture the eye of anyone. It was really a nice-sized house.

"Dang Moke... is this where you live?"

"Yes, but only because of our father, who happens to be an officer."

"An officer. Like a police officer?"

"Yes. Our father has done great providing for us and has been an officer for as long as I can remember. Vincent, you've been pursued, either by local, state, or federal law for as long as we've known each other, so there was never a good time to explain to you that my dad was a cop. It could have ruined our friendship, and that means the world to me.

"Come on, let's go inside," he said, reaching for the door.

Upon entering, we made our way into the living room, where his mother met us with a smile.

"Hello, son, come in."

"Hey, Mama, I'd like you to meet my friend. This is Vincent."

"Hi, Vincent! I just put on a fresh pot of coffee. Go to the kitchen and have a seat at the table. It's cold out. I'll pour both of you a cup."

In the kitchen, she asked, "So, Vincent, how are you, and how long will you be visiting with us?"

"Not long. We're headed to New York."

"New York! Moke, does that mean you're not staying?"

He crossed his arms and sucked through his teeth. It was hard telling your mother after just arriving that you wouldn't be staying. "No, ma'am, I'm going to live with Madea."

He had mentioned some time back that he didn't know how his grandmother could afford to stay in New York, but every time they talked, she would always ask him to come live with her. He had also said previously that she had been trying to get his dad to leave South Carolina as well, always telling him that he was risking his life working for "slave money."

"Son!" she yelled, apparently a little disgusted. "Your dad will be disappointed. You had promised to join the church. Plus, there's a lot going on around here right now."

"What's wrong?" he asked as if there were something he could do.

"People are being forced to move out of their homes, and finding somewhere for all of them to go is difficult," she said tentatively.

"So, are they giving you a reason?" he asked as he unfolded his arms to take a sip of his coffee.

"Not one that everybody understands and is willing to live with, but what's known to be fact is that the government has purchased the land in the lower area of Pine. Something about an urban renewal project. Moke, everyone who is left in that Gas Bottom community will have to move. We get it, though, being one of the worst slums in our city and the only section left from when people were forced out in the early sixties. But where will all these people go? Son, I have been a city activist ever since experiencing similar treatment when you were a kid. We, too, had to move out from the Gas Bottom community, but this time, not even I can fix it. It's overwhelming, and there's nowhere to place so many deprived families.

"Come, we should have a seat in the living room. It's a lot more comfortable."

"Where's my sister?" Moke asked as we entered the living room.

"On her way home. She's trying to get accepted into the community college."

"Well, how is that going?"

Suddenly, we heard the door open, and I watched as his sister walked through. He only managed a couple of steps toward her before she leaped into his arms. His mother and I stood and watched as they embraced.

"Man! You're finally home. How long will you be here, and who's your friend?" she asked with a high-pitched voice as she observed my appearance.

"Bee-Bee, this is Vincent, the guy I've been telling you about."

Then Moke's mother spoke. "I'm going back to the kitchen. None of y'all leave without eating something."

"Yes, ma'am," Moke answered.

"Huh! So, you're the fellow he calls Smooth."

"Oh, he does?"

"Yes."

"That's new, 'cause I've never heard him call me that."

"Maybe he doesn't to you, but when he mentions your name in our conversations, it doesn't seem to be Vincent. Listen, I got-ta get cleaned up. My friend Lilah is picking me up. Smooth, I'll get with you later. Moke, how long will you be home?"

"I'm not sure. I'll tell you once I discuss it with Dad."

"Cool, I'm out. Hey, it's Friday! New Year's Eve. Y'all should come to the party with us tonight. What you think, Vincent?"

I believe Bee-Bee stunned her brother with that gesture, but I quickly shot back, "Sure. Just leave the address with Moke. Once I have a decent room secured and am settled in, I'll give it some thought."

"Okay," she said, hunching her shoulders as she continued upstairs.

"Damn, Moke! What happened to you? Your sister is pretty cool."

"Yes, she is! Bee-Bee and Lilah have been best friends since they were in grade school. Lilah's mother is a schoolteacher, and her father is a local minister and our family pastor. Her father and our dad are also good friends, and from what we grew up knowing, her father is no regular round-da-corner, Oral Roberts-type minister. This dude was a gangster. We heard he once blew up a place while in the military. We've also been told he did time on a charge of conspiracy to commit robbery and kidnap, but that was overturned by an appeal. Actually, all the old ladies in our neighborhood church love him. Vincent, this guy is one heck of a preacher."

"The food is ready. You both come and get something to eat."

Neither of us was hungry. On our way, we had eaten every damn kind of junk food in sight, but we had to please his mom. Afterward, he rode with me to the motel close by the railroad tracks, not far from their neighborhood. On the way, I asked Moke, "Hey, dude, what about your sister and her friend? Are they dating anybody?"

"No, not that I know of. Bee-Bee has lots of male friends 'cause of where we grew up, but Lilah, her dad has always kept a close eye on her. She could rarely come play with Bee. I would have to walk with her over to Lilah's house for them to play with each other until they got big. Even when Lilah started driving, she would have to come pick Bee up, and they would ride back to her house."

Cutting my eyes sharply at him, I asked, "Hey man, what the hell is this?"

"What?"

"This place, what is this?"

"It's the motel we all have to use."

"Maybe y'all... Heck, take me to a better spot. This one should be condemned."

"But, Vincent, you won't be accepted in on the far end of town."

At that point, my entire demeanor took on a subtle change. I pulled into the next filling station and grabbed my bag from the back seat. We both walked inside, and I asked the attendant for the restroom key. He gave it to us, and we went around the building to find the restroom. Moke waited while standing in front of the Monte Carlo.

There I stood before closing the restroom door behind me, my reflection in the mirror fully dressed in an officer's military uniform, complete with a cap and insignia. Afterward, I walked quickly back to the car.

"Let's go," I said quickly but in a gentler tone. "Show me where it is."

"Show you what?" he asked with a nervous expression.

"A nice hotel, an expensive one, if you don't mind."

He was frightened and trembling but did what I asked.

"Wait in the car," I told him when we pulled up, and I entered what looked to be one of the finest hotels in town. "Miss, could I get a room, please? I'm on orders from the Army Reserve Center. I'll be here for a few days, if not a week."

"Your name, sir?"

"Lieutenant Goldsby."

"Sign here, and we'll get you taken care of."

Just like that, I was in and out with no problem, almost like I was a White guy, and we were headed back to Moke's house.

"Damn, Vincent! How'd you do that?" Moke asked, knowing I wasn't supposed to be wearing that uniform.

"Moke, it's the respect one receives while in the military. They don't care what you look like. They only see the color of the uniform. Hey! I remember Bee-Bee inviting us to a party. You be ready when I get back."

"Man, I cannot believe you're going back to that hotel," he said with fear. "But don't worry, I'll be ready if you make it back."

Lilah and Bee-Bee had already left when I showed up, but with their directions, we made it to the party with everything in motion. With the likes of Teddy Pendergrass's "Wake Up Everybody" spinning, everyone was bobbing and weaving their heads.

That's when I noticed her. Lilah. It had to be her, the person standing with Bee-Bee. It was, and she was beautiful, radiant and thick-boned, a medium light skin person with a perfect petite waist. They both were gorgeous.

Chapter 2. Home from School

This chapter is told through the viewpoint of Lilah and is based on a conversation that took place between her and Bee-Bee, one that happened way too late in life. While Bee-Bee was telling the story to me, I could almost feel the deep hurt and disloyalty she had endured, having to live through countless years of suffering without a person who felt so dear because of a highly deceitful act of betrayal that took place over a couple of decades and damaged a friendship to the point of no recovery.

After many years, Lilah was finally ready to describe to her old friend what had happened. It was an intricate story involving a number of people, people she held dear and was determined to protect. While her initial scheme was successful and, to her mind, genuinely justified, what seemed best for Lilah at the time had a damaging effect on others. It was a disastrous event for all, especially Bee-Bee, who at that time was considered her best friend. After years of selfishness, Lilah's conscience finally weakened to the point she could barely live with herself anymore for what she had done, and she decided to confess everything—from her first irresponsible mistake to all the many bad and stupid choices she made thereafter.

Looking back at Lilah's story...

"Bee-Bee, who is that? He doesn't look to be from around here."

She adjusted her glasses to get a better look. "Oh, him? He's my brother's friend, the guy he came home with."

"The one you call 'Smooth'?"

"Hello, ladies!" he said in a lovely Southern accent.

"Lilah, this is Vincent, the one I was telling you about," Bee-Bee said with an attitude, and I could see why. He was handsome, with black curly hair and beautiful light-brown skin, but there was something different about him, too. The way he looked, he seemed to be undressing me, and his attention had me wet.

I didn't need that. I was already thinking about what I should do about... down there.

He was well dressed, with a small but semi-muscular body, and I loved a guy with naturally curly hair. His clothes looked expensive. He was wearing a black double-breasted velvet jacket with a pair of black-and-white Stacy Adams shoes. The man looked like money, but something more—he brought a vibe with him I'd never felt before. I then adjusted my glasses and stuck my index finger into my mouth. I was about to melt.

"You're beautiful, Bee-Bee," he said, while politely kissing her forehead. He then reached out and took my hand, giving it a passionate kiss. "How are you, Lilah? It's truly a pleasure to finally meet after hearing so much about you. I heard you were at South Carolina State, home of the mighty Bulldogs. How is it there?"

"School's great, and I'm actually an honor student." But school was the last thing on my mind. "Smooth, huh? Can I call you that?"

"Sure. I don't have a problem with it," he said. The way he had moved toward me, greeted me, kissed my hand... it all had me shivering with excitement.

"So how long will you be in town, Smooth?" I asked with more concern than anyone could know, even Bee-Bee.

"I'm not sure, Lilah, but meeting you could have a great impact on how that goes. Look, why don't I get you ladies something to drink? What would you like?"

"I don't drink," said Bee-Bee.

"No problem. I'll be right back with something you both will enjoy."

When he was gone, I turned to Bee-Bee. "*Gurrrl*, why didn't you tell me he looked like that?"

"Heck, Lilah, you've never shown any interest in men."

Between Smooth's introduction and my little secret, my mind started racing. *What if sneaking over to my professor's house that one time made me pregnant? 'Cause I haven't seen my period at all this month. Shucks! I hope not, 'cause it wasn't even good. Damn! I'm standing here perspiring all over myself, and this guy Smooth has only spoken to me. I can only imagine what making love really feels like.*

I cannot be pregnant. I just can't be. I don't even have a boyfriend. What am I supposed to do? My mom is going to kill me. An abortion is out of the question with her. Could I be overreacting? Maybe! But this is a chance I cannot take. I have to do something. He's my professor. I need a plan.

"Lilah, are you okay?" Bee-Bee asked. "You don't look well. Can I get you something?"

She was thinking the excitement of the lovely greeting had my body struggling to keep cool. That was only part of it. This nausea, the body temperature, and the perspiration were probably the result of an untimely pregnancy.

"No, Bee-Bee, but you can give Smooth my number and tell him if he likes, he can call me tomorrow. You're right, something's come over me. Please apologize for my leaving so abruptly."

On my way home, I started to feel faint, but I managed to get myself to the hospital. Once inside the double doors, I fell to my knees. The last thing I heard before blacking out was the medical clerk calling for assistance.

***

"Hello, Miss Bryant. I'm Dr. Paula. How're you feeling?" the doctor asked as she finished her examination.

"I'm feeling much better, but what happened? Why am I here?"

"You were admitted after bringing yourself to the emergency room. If it hadn't been for your student ID, we wouldn't have been able to identify you. Your parents are on their way."

"Will I be all right?"

"Certainly. You should be fine, and your baby seems to be healthy as well."

Baby! That confirms my suspicion about why I missed my period.

Seeing my expression, the physician said, "You're five weeks into your pregnancy. Did you not know?"

My thoughts were all over the damn place, and I didn't hear a word the doctor said. "I'm sorry, what did you say?"

"Miss Bryant, you're five weeks pregnant. Congratulations!"

"Thanks," I replied, but there was nothing I could do to soothe the apprehension I had over telling my parents.

"Doc, did you say my parents are on their way?"

"Yes, they were contacted a little over fifteen minutes ago and should be arriving any minute now."

"Dr. Paula, is it possible you could not tell my parents that I'm pregnant? They don't know, and I would like to figure this out and be the one to tell them. Could you do that for me, please?"

Dr. Paula must have seen this many times before because she knew exactly what to do.

"Yes, Lilah. Can I call you by your first name?"

"Yes, ma'am. Please just don't tell them."

"Don't worry, you are of age, and it's your decision. We couldn't inform them if we wanted to."

The doctor calmed me down with her reassurance. Then my parents entered the room, asking questions. She told them I was fine, that I had overheated and was diagnosed with dehydration, which caused me to faint.

My mother stood by my bedside, comforting me until my release. My father stood talking with the doctor by the doorway, trying to pry what he could out of her while I listened very carefully, hoping the doctor had been honest about what she had promised me.

"Dr. Paula, anything else that you may be able to tell me about my daughter? Is there any illness that could cause dizziness? For her to collapse like that..."

"Sir, she's okay. Just make sure she eats properly and drinks lots of fluids. We found no medical issues, so don't worry. Your daughter is fine."

***

The next day when the phone rang, I found myself thinking, *Man, I hope this is him.*

"Lilah, please."

"This is she. Who's asking?"

"This is Vincent, and I'm sorry if I did something to upset you. If so, I'd like to apologize."

"You? No, man. I'm the one who should be apologizing. I'm sorry for leaving so suddenly. I'd like to make it up to you if you're willing to accept."

This guy has already mentioned his stay here could depend on me. Maybe I should use that to my advantage. My professor will be in deep trouble if I don't come up with some type of plan. Plus, I really would like to make it up to him, though I'm not sure he even likes me after disappearing like I did last night.

"Lilah, I was under the impression I had done something to offend you. Since that isn't the case, are you okay?"

"Yes, I'm fine."

"Then what do you have to ask me?"

"My mother has been selected for Teacher of the Year honors. Would you like to attend the gala presentation with me next Saturday? It starts at seven thirty. Also, it would be nice if you would be able to have Sunday dinner with us tomorrow." *Am I being too forward? Could I be pushing this chance away? Lord, I have no choice... nobody can find out that the professor is the father of my child.*

"Yes to both of your questions! I'd love to, and I appreciate your offer. What time should I be there?"

"One o'clock should be fine. Dinner is usually served around two."

"One o'clock it is. Are you sure you're okay?"

"Yes, I'm good. Hope to see you soon."

Chapter 3. Pastor Bryant's Secrets

When I realized after hanging up with Lilah that I didn't have her address, I called Bee-Bee. After telling her about the invitation, I gathered that whether I would get a chance to attend the gala would be determined in part by my appearance and performance at the dinner. After pulling up to their home and stepping out of the Monte Carlo, I brushed off my clothing to make sure there was no trace of lint.

Finally, I made my way to the house and rang their doorbell.

"I'll get it!" I heard Lilah's voice call out. A moment later, she was opening the door. "Vincent! You're looking very conservative."

"I was hoping it would be appropriate. You look stunning."

"Come in. My father is waiting. Daddy!"

"Over here, Lilah." We found her father in the den, standing in front of a large portrait of himself.

"Good evening, sir. How are you?" I said, offering Pastor Bryant a firm handshake.

"Hello, son. How do you know my daughter, and what brings you to Spartanburg?"

Her father's first words were abrupt, but true to my name, I played it smooth. "I met her through Bee-Bee. Her brother Moke and I are close friends. I'm here visiting their family for a while. I'm not sure yet how long I'll be staying."

Her mother interrupted, letting us know dinner was ready. After we were all seated, her father said grace, but soon after, he was into me again.

I'll never make it to the gala, the way this guy is drilling me. What is up with him?

"Okay, Vincent. Since you're not sure of the length of your stay, then where will you be staying?"

"The hotel near the railroad tracks. My stay hasn't been as comfortable as expected, but I'm making the best of it. I'm from Louisiana, sir, where you are taught to make the best of whatever is presented to you. The hotel may not be the nicest, but I can live with that."

Her father was prying, but my answers were right on point. Not only did I look the part, but I was coming off as very witty and intelligent.

"Vincent," Mrs. Bryant said, "where are you headed once your stay is over?"

"To New York, Mrs. Bryant. I found a school that I'm told is the best in the country, and I would like to attend it."

"What type, may I ask?"

"Sure, I would like to be a private investigator."

"Oh, is that right? Why a private investigator?" Mrs. Bryant had questions too, but they didn't come with the same aggression as Pastor Bryant's.

"Mrs. Bryant, there's something thrilling about doing investigative research and watching your creative package come to fruition. Oh, by the way—I just finished an office administration business course a few months back, and it will help in managing my affairs once things are up in running. I'm doing my best to get my career started early."

"That is magnificent and sounds impressive, Vincent. I'm proud of you."

"Thank you. Lilah has mentioned how successful you've been in your teaching career. You must be proud of yourself for your achievements. They seem astronomical."

"Yes, I am, and thank you for your kind words. They mean a lot. Would you care for anything else? Maybe some more tea?"

"No, I'm good, but a small piece of dessert would be fine."

"Coming right up."

***

The family dinner had gone well, so well that her mother asked, "Vincent, did Lilah invite you to the school's gala next weekend? I would love to have you attend the event with us."

"Yes, ma'am, she did mention it, and I would love nothing more than to escort her to the gala."

Lilah's dad wasn't buying into my charm, not nearly in the fashion of her mother, though he did coast along. As the dinner progressed, Lilah's confidence level continued to grow. She became intrigued to find out more about me. I had held my own through what was a wonderful meal capped with a delicious dessert. Succeeding a very delicious piece of pie, her mother suggested we move to the den for a quick game of Scrabble.

As we resumed, I noticed Pastor Bryant constantly squeezing his nose as if cleaning the outer surface. He repeated this process several times with a handkerchief. He wasn't saying much as Lilah, her mother, and I continued to battle each other with words. Their backs were to him, and he was looking dubious of me.

***

The following Thursday, after finishing a delicious breakfast at the Skillet restaurant down on the corner of East Main and South Pine, I drove back to the luxury hotel on the other end of town. The lobby was thinning out from the early morning departures, so I walked over to take a seat at one of the empty tables to finish reading the morning paper. Afterward, I decided to return to my room.

As I stood, two men entered the hotel lobby from the opposite end of the building. As they passed by, one of them dropped his handkerchief.

"Sir!" I called out. "Here, you dropped this."

9

Surely, his back was to me, he was dressed differently and wore dark rim glasses, but when he blinked himself out of his stupor and reached for the handkerchief, I could tell it was him. Mr. Bryant, I was sure of it. I took it they were at some type of conference or having a business meeting.

"Thanks," he said, clearly trying to figure out if I were someone he knew. Yes, the military uniform may have thrown him off, but he showed complete obliviousness as if under some form of drug or in a state of shock. It definitely wasn't alcohol because he didn't seem to be physically impaired, and it was nine o'clock on a Thursday morning. The smell of that handkerchief, however, gave off all the warning signs of cocaine.

We all turned and walked toward the elevator and waited for it to open. Upon entering, I stood behind them so as not to be scrutinized. We all got off on the second floor, and I stopped at the ice machine for a moment in order to see where they were going—down the hall a couple of rooms to the right of the elevator.

I had the last room on the same side of the hall. I returned there to brush my teeth and clean out the remaining particles of my wonderful breakfast. Then I changed out of the military uniform into something more casual to take a stroll, maybe to the city park.

It all happened simultaneously. I saw Mr. Bryant and his friend leaving, this time with a briefcase, one he did not have when he was downstairs.

A cleaning lady was finishing up the room across from them and happened to be opening the door they had just exited.

While holding a fifty-dollar bill in my hand, I said to her, "Miss, that room you're getting ready to clean... could you tell me who occupies it?"

She was hesitant, but after looking at the fifty and slowly reaching for it, she replied, "I don't know who."

"Do you know either of the men who just departed?"

"Yes. Pastor Bryant from the large church. He meets here once every other month or so."

This dude cannot be dealing, I thought. "Are there ever any females meeting with him?"

"I'm not sure. I've never witnessed any."

I slid her another fifty bucks for cooperating. *I can see why he never separated from that scarf while at dinner the other night.*

"And you're sure you don't know the other guy?"

"No, I don't."

After getting all I could from the housekeeper, I hurried downstairs, hoping it was quicker than using the elevator. It was. Pastor Bryant was just closing the door after placing the briefcase on the back seat of his BMW. After positioning himself under the wheel to leave, he pulled out onto Main Street, unaware he was being followed. He drove across town to exactly where the housekeeper had mentioned a huge church sitting on a corner block all to itself. The pastor made a left turn into what looked to be the congregation's parking lot, but instead of parking in his designated spot, he exited the car to lift up a private garage door that perfectly matched the structure of the building and was barely recognizable. He then proceeded to pull into the building and shut the garage door behind him. From the way it looked, he wanted his presence inside known to no one.

From the very first time the pastor and I met, there was something strange about him, first from his interrogation of me, then the sniffing of the handkerchief at dinner that I noticed for a second time in the hotel lobby. The handkerchief let off a strong metallic, chemical scent, an odor that would suggest the use of excessive amounts of cocaine.

Shit. You didn't have to be particularly smart to tell something was up with Pastor Bryant. Aside from his handkerchief and secret parking garage, there was something else noticeable and very unusual: at no point did he ever carry his Bible, just a briefcase, and very rarely does a pastor stick his Bible inside a carrying case.

I followed him, making the same turns but keeping straight when he took the first lift, parking in a separate lot across the street, far away from his church. It may have been safer and out of the way of being seen by anyone, but I needed to be closer. While sitting trying to figure this shit out, I removed from my pouch a mini-drug spoon and a small fifty-dollar plastic bag of TAC. After snorting two good scoops into each nostril, my mind began to click.

It registered. I had a Slim Jim stashed in my trunk under the mat. Wasting no time, I grabbed it and slipped it between my arm and body. I then crossed the street and found a small gap in the garage door. I was able to raise the door, and less than a minute later, I slid the tool down the window of the driver's side door. The lock clicked, the door opened, and I was in.

I found nothing. After rifling through his possessions, all I produced was a pack of Top rolling papers, which led me to believe whatever he got from that hotel must be in the church.

Once he left the building for the day, I would find out, but not in broad daylight. My plan was to wait until dark, well after he had departed the premises. With nothing else to do, I returned to the hotel and spoke to Anita, asking her to put me down for a 6:00 p.m. wake-up, just in case.

I proceeded to my room, changed clothes, and lounged around watching television until I fell asleep. Once I was up and awake, the time had come, but first I stopped by the Sugar-n-Spice drive in and ordered a fish plate served with fries. After finishing what turned out to be a great meal sent down with a large glass of sweet tea, I traveled the same route back to the church.

Thoroughly checking each door, I found what appeared to be the only door without a deadbolt—the main entrance to his church.

Damn! I thought.

The light in front of the church was bright, and this was by far the most lit-up area, but it happened to be the easiest lock to pick.

Whoever orchestrated this one-lock system had given me confidence, in spite of the powerful outside lighting. They didn't seem to factor in that it wouldn't take long to pick one lock. I proceeded with the task at hand, knowing if someone were to suddenly pass by it could be dangerous for me. But that was a chance I had to take, and anyway, I had taken note of the low traffic count, so my confidence level had risen high that I could pick the lock and be inside before anyone noticed.

Upon entering his church, which was quite large, the process of finding his safe wasn't as hard as I initially thought considering I only had a small flashlight that barely put out enough light to get around. After shoving the office door open, I found the same large portrait of himself he had hanging on his living room wall. "Umm," I said aloud as I walked toward it. "What a coincidence." I moved it to one side and found a medium-sized wall safe hiding behind it.

His safe was new and impeccably secure. Its unique qualities had me brainstorming all my abilities, but with just a few minor issues and little to no damage, it opened. Afterward, what I found sitting inside was something surprising even to me. There were ten plastic bags filled with white powder. I reached into my front pocket and pulled out my pocketknife to dab a small hole into one of them. It was obvious to me what it was, but I needed to know the extent of its potency. No doubt it was some of the finest cocaine Spartanburg had to offer. Also, sitting just to the right of those double stacks of five was a fully compressed brick and three ounces of some of the best-smelling weed in the southern part of the country. All I took was one bag of his cocaine and one ounce of weed. With that, I left his safe door wide open, a hint for him to be careful.

Chapter 4. Saturday's Gala

"Vincent!" Mrs. Bryant greeted me. "You're early."

"Yes, ma'am. I thought maybe the pastor and I could squeeze in a few minutes of conversation before leaving for the gala." I was curious to know if he suspected it was me who handed him that handkerchief Thursday morning.

"I'm glad you could make it. I'm on my way out to the gala. Please, have a seat. I'll inform Lilah you're here. Oh, and the pastor was in his study, and I'm not sure he hasn't left already."

"Thanks, Mrs. Bryant, and I must say, you look amazing." She looked over her shoulder, smiling as she continued upstairs. Several minutes later, Lilah entered the den wrapped in an old winter-type duster, a robe that looked to belong to her grandmother.

"Hi, Vincent. Mother told me you were here before she left. I'll turn the TV on for you, and don't worry, I'll be ready shortly."

As she started up the stairs, I couldn't help but ask, "Lilah! What do you have on under there?"

"Would you really like to know?"

Is she seriously asking me that?

"Here!" she said, removing one side of the heavy cloth robe and showing a portion of her beautifully shaped thigh.

"Damn! Where's your daddy?" I asked, grasping right away that he, too, must be gone.

"He left a little before my mom. Headed to his church. He said he'd meet us at the gala. Would you like to come up while I finish getting dressed?"

Shit! Her father could be busy for a while, I thought, *especially if he's at the church, because there's no way he hasn't discovered what happened.* Her question went unanswered as I followed her up the stairs.

Man, what the fuck? Once we entered her bedroom, all decked out in pink and green décor, she turned her radio on and walked toward the bathroom. "I'll be right out, Vincent," she teased. "Unless you want to come in with me…"

My man was hard as cement. As she entered the bathroom, I grabbed both elastic trims of her panties and popped her checks with them. While she ran the water for her bath, I eased behind her nearly naked body with my arms wrapped around her, hands massaging her breasts, going in from beneath her arms and moving my hands slowly up and down the front of her smooth body, from her lovely breasts down between her expensive panties to her twat.

Pulling her gently backward with me while listening to the running water from the faucet, I calmly sat on the toilet seat. Then she sat on top of me, her legs straddled to the sides while I smothered my head between her boobs, teasing her from there to the flesh of her nipples.

She began to get hot and started kissing me with every bit of energy she had. I began removing her panties while gently standing her up, placing her body toward the wall with the palms of her hands in the air. All in one motion while leaning on the back of her butt, I turned off the water. I proceeded with both hands to softly rub her thick thighs from behind in a circular motion, finally working my way to her overly hairy slit I started to massage it with the tip of my index fingers and could feel the sensation as it slowly hardened.

My temperature began to rise, and my man was beginning to explode. She backed away from the wall and bent over. While teasing her with the head of my cock, I started to spread her clit using both my thumbs. She was not stopping me, so I turned her away from the wall while still spreading her thighs wider and grabbing her arms, placing them down inside the tub, her knees on the floor and her face nearly touching the water. I licked her from the bend of her knee to the very center of her split.

She began to get very wet, moaning and letting me know not to stop. By now, I was out of all my clothes. My man was about to burst as I started to move it toward her spot, teasing her in and out and in every way feasible. She pushed away from the tub with one hand and reached between her legs with the other. She grabbed my shaft and started to stroke it like it had never been before. While stroking my man with one hand, she completely backed me up. After removing herself from the tub, she placed both hands flat on the floor, balancing herself on all fours and asking me to place it inside her.

"Are you sure?" I asked. "Are you really ready?"

"Yes, Smooth, yes!" she cried out. "Now!"

"Lilah, I don't want to hurt you."

"It's okay," she moaned as I slid in the head of my dick, teasing and playing at the very tip of her twat. "It feels good. In, Smooth. In a little more."

I pushed in a little deeper, and she was adjusting to it as it swelled larger. Finally, it was in, all in, all of it. Suddenly, we heard a knock downstairs. I pulled out, never reaching the pinnacle point. "Who can that be?" she asked, moving naked to her bedroom window to see.

"Who is it?" I asked.

"I couldn't really tell," she whispered, "but it looked to be Bee-Bee walking away."

Soon she was back in the bathroom, over by the tub, to top off what had gotten cool with some hot running water and continue with her bath. "Vincent, would you like to join me? I don't think we have enough time for separate baths."

It appeared she lost that lusting desire she once had for me, though we were running short on time. After finishing our bath, we got dressed and left for the gala.

"Vincent, is *that* why they call you Smooth?" she asked as we rode to the gala.

"No! Is that what you think?"

She shrugged her shoulders. "You seem experienced. I thought maybe you do it to all the women you meet."

"No, Lilah! When you jokingly opened the robe, your body was perfect, and from the minute we met, it's been like we've known each other for life. The timing seemed right, and the opportunity was there." *What was I supposed to have done?* I thought.

We made it to the gala right as the host speaker started to address the crowd. We grabbed our seats next to Lilah's father. He gave us a look that said, *What the hell have you two been up to?* I don't think he cared very much for me because of the speed at which I had his daughter traveling. And not only the speed—she'd never had a boyfriend, from what I had been told.

Bee-Bee elbowed me in the side and whispered, "Let's switch seats." She wanted to sit next to Lilah.

"Gurrrl, you are glowing. What did y'all do?" I could hear her whispering to Lilah, but she only smiled and pointed her thumb back over her shoulder to her father.

"You have to tell me everything," is what I could decipher from Bee-Bee as she whispered a second time. She turned and glanced at me.

"What?" I asked, giving her a smirk.

And I was thinking that to Lilah's father as well for the facial expression he was giving me. Looking at him from the corner of my eye, it was obvious he wasn't enjoying himself, probably due to the fact his cocaine was missing. He must have been trying to figure out who in hell would break into his safe, take one ounce of his shit, and leave the safe door wide open. And, to top it all off, he had to watch his sweet precious princess run around town with some punk nobody knew. His expression toward me was the first intimation that he could have some perception of what had actually happened.

Mrs. Bryant spoke well as she received the teacher of the year award, and afterward, we all gathered around as the event came to a close. I watched as everyone took their turn congratulating Mrs. Bryant; Bee-Bee was the only one who showed no interest. She was more into finding out what happened with Lilah, but she was riding with me, which made it difficult for the two of them to engage in a conversation.

Once we got in the Monte Carlo, I heard Bee-Bee tell Lilah, "Tomorrow I'll be calling you," giving a phone gesture with her pinky finger and thumb.

We then returned to their home.

Chapter 5. Lilah's Situation

Again, told through the viewpoint of Lilah...

As promised, the phone rang the next morning, and I hurried downstairs to answer it. We only had one, and it was in the den sitting on our beautiful Hawthorne table.

"Wake up, gurrrl," Bee-Bee said.

"What, Bee-Bee?" I turned over to look at the clock on the wall—6:30 a.m. "Bee-Bee, it's early. I'm just getting up. But if you're going to ask me about last night when you knocked on our door and I didn't answer, then I'm up."

"What happened? Tell me everything. Every detail."

"Bee-Bee, he's amazing, and we had the best time ever. Girl, he bent me over backward and broke me off. Bee, you have got to try it. I know you haven't yet, but this feeling is better than anything else in the world."

"How'd you know what to do?"

"I didn't have to. He made it easy for me."

Bee-Bee got quiet for a moment. "Was it really that good?"

"It was excellent! He was very passionate, and sexy, and he broke me off. I didn't plan on giving him a kiss, much less make love to him."

"Well, dang!" she yelled. I had her believing it was my first time, and I meant to keep it that way. She was my best friend, but she couldn't know about the humiliating mistake I'd made with the professor. I'd known Bee-Bee forever. I knew her ways. I wasn't sure she would be able to keep it a secret. "Will you be seeing him again?"

"No, I won't. He's leaving for New York soon, he said. Plus, I have to go back to college."

"You must get his address."

"I'm not sure of that. What if he doesn't care to see me again?"

"Gurl, you crazy. The man just removed your panties. I know if it were me, surely I would want to see him again. You should get his number, or better yet—give him yours."

"Lilah!" my father called.

"I have to go—my dad just called."

I hung up as he came into the room. "Lilah, how much do you know about this young man?"

I rolled my eyes and shook my head, knowing he was getting ready to interrogate me. This is why I couldn't have a boyfriend—because he would run them all away. "Daddy, he's nice, respectable, and I like him."

"Sweetheart, you know nothing about him, and from what I'm told, he's only been in town for a week. Where's he staying, and with whom? He surely doesn't live with Moke senior, so do you even know?"

Actually, I didn't know. My situation was putting so much pressure on me that focusing on where he was staying wasn't a concern. I needed a daddy for my baby, and that was all that mattered. He said the Motel by the railroad tracks, and I took his word for that.

"Lilah, we had a very unusual situation at the church last week, and I need you to stay away from this guy. I mean it."

"But, Daddy, what could he have to do with what happened at your church? He probably doesn't even know where your church is."

"Someone told me his vehicle was seen in the neighborhood of the church earlier last week."

"Really, Daddy? Your church is off Main Street. What's unusual about that? And why did it have to be his car?"

"Because I'm told it's the only one like it in town—a black Monte Carlo that has large whitewall tires."

"Daddy, if it was his car, did they get a look at his license plate? How can they be so sure? This town is not that small."

"Just stay away from him. That's an order."

I did, and for several days, I had no communication with anyone. But as my situation continued to develop for the worse, I decided to call Bee-Bee.

"What is going on?" she asked. "Are you crying?"

I tried to compose myself, but I was too upset. "My dad wants me to stay away from Smooth, but I really like him."

"Why would he tell you that?" Bee-Bee's concern was sincere. I had her believing it was the truth.

"I'm not sure. Something happened at his church, and someone was supposed to have seen Smooth's car in that area."

"Any proof of him doing anything? Because that's a long way from where Moke said he was staying. He's on the opposite end of town from where your father's church sits. Although once he leaves from over there, he does have to pass by the church, so it's possible his car could have been seen on Main Street. But that doesn't mean anything, and it definitely doesn't prove he had anything to do with what happened at your dad's church."

"Well, I'm confused. How could he get a room across town? Only wealthy or prominent people are welcome over there."

"Dang, girl, you have to admit—the guy is rather unique."

"Sure. I can attest to that. But none of it makes sense. What does where he stays have to do with my daddy's church?"

"I don't know. Maybe there's a reason, and your father really needs to know. Or perhaps he's just coming up with something to keep you guys apart."

"You're probably right—something he's always done. Where's Moke? Is he there? Do you think he might know something?"

"I'm not sure, but even if he doesn't, it's worth a try. Wait, I'll get him. Moke! Lilah wants to speak with you! She's on the phone!"

Moke picked up. "Hello?"

"Look, man—do you think your friend had anything to do with what happened at my dad's church?"

"What happened at his church?"

"I don't know, but he said someone saw your friend's car in the neighborhood."

"Heck, Lilah, he's a highly active guy, but if it were my guess, I would say no. But with him, anything's possible. I will say this to you—I've been around him for a while, and I know he doesn't do things randomly or without a plan. If by chance he or his vehicle was seen in that area, I wouldn't doubt at all if your dad were behind him being there."

"Dude, is he really that smooth?"

"His nickname... it's an understatement. But if this serves as any consolation, I wouldn't worry about him. What I do know is he wouldn't do anything to offend you or your family. But knowing how your father operates, I wouldn't put it past him to try and help your dad in some form."

How could that be? He doesn't know my dad. "The only interaction between those two was at our house for dinner. They seriously don't know one another."

"Lilah, he's a guy who rarely sits still, and if his vehicle being observed in that area is something of significance to your dad, then something must have happened. But that only means his interest led him to the area. It doesn't mean he knows or did anything wrong."

Could he be right? "Then what do you suggest?"

"Humm. I wouldn't worry so much. Both of you guys are leaving town soon. Things should settle down, and your father will stop pestering you."

"You must really know him."

"Who? Your father?"

"No, silly," she said, laughing. "Smooth."

Chapter 6. Overly Aggressive Harassment

A week after the gala on an early Sunday morning, I slowly made my way down the street where Lilah's family lived. As I gradually approached their house, I could see her dad's car was missing from the driveway. If her father weren't at home, it would be a great opportunity for me to let her know I was leaving town.

Before I could press the doorbell, the door opened.

"Vincent!" Lilah said. "I didn't know you were out here."

"I was about to ring."

"Man, how are you?"

"I'm decent. How's it going with you?"

"Who's at the door?" her mom asked as she leaned against the door frame.

"It's Vincent!" she yelled back.

"Let him in!"

"Look, I've gathered that your father doesn't care much for me. Therefore, I'm only here to let you know I'll be leaving for New York right after I holler at Moke."

"Okay, but at least come inside. It wouldn't hurt to say something to my mom before you leave. If you don't, she's going to be disappointed."

I couldn't see anything wrong with that, so I did. "Lilah, once I get settled, is there a number where you can be reached?" I asked while standing and admiring the beauty of the designs stitched deep into their plush white living room carpet.

Her mother bounced down the stairs and walked into the room, looking radiant as ever. She stood there a moment, beautiful, but with an uncanny, mysterious type of look. Then she gave me a welcoming smile I would remember for a lifetime.

"How are you, Vincent?" she asked.

"I'm decent, Mrs. Bryant, though I'm only here to let you guys know I'm leaving today."

"That's great. I'm glad you stopped by. Anytime you're in the area, remember you're always welcome."

"Thanks, Mrs. Bryant. I'll remember that."

I believed Mrs. Bryant knew much more about her husband's actions than she'd be willing to admit. Still, she maintained a dignified mien, in spite of them. Using the accolades and awards she'd received over the years during a successful teaching career, to keep her gracious and down-to-earth.

"You're welcome, Vincent! Now, a little hug before you go, and you remember what I said."

As she climbed the stairs again and disappeared, I couldn't help thinking there was something different about her. As if she could see straight through my attractive and fascinating charm, that it was something more beneath such an alluring face. Her husband and daughter were in distress about what happened at the church, yet she was unsentimental and fervent towards me. I thought, maybe she was enjoying what happened to Pastor Bryant. Here's my number at school, Vincent. I reached for it, the fragrance from my cologne must have reminded her of that magnificent evening we shared together. Before I could utter the word thanks, she kissed me.

"Does that mean goodbye?" I asked as she backed away.

"Yes, Mr. Smooth," she said with a delightful smile, "because I'll probably never see you again."

"No, Lilah! I'll see you on campus in a few weeks."

"Sure, Vincent, but not likely."

"I got you," I said, not quite in agreement with her statement. I spoke with confidence because I knew in a few weeks I would find a way to see her.

***

It wasn't long after leaving Lilah that I saw the red and blue lights flashing in the rearview mirror. *Man, what-ta these folks want?* I asked myself as the cops pulled me over before reaching Moke's house.

"License and registration, please," the officer asked.

What the heck can this be about? "Here, sir. And why am I being stopped?"

"Do you realize you're supposed to come to a complete stop when approaching a stop sign?"

"Yes, sir," I answered respectfully. "I do, and I'm quite sure of myself that I did."

"There's a very strange odor coming from inside. Could you step out of the car, please?"

"Sure!" I wasn't going back and forth with these guys. I'd just do what I was told.

"Would it be all okay with you if we searched your vehicle?"

"Shouldn't you have a search warrant to do that?"

"Only if you decline."

I thought quickly. I wasn't hiding anything, so I agreed and politely asked, "What is it you guys are looking for?"

"Anything that could be causing the odor that has alarmed us. Have you been smoking or drinking anything?"

"No, sir. I haven't."

Soon after answering his question, it dawned on me that something else was wrong. This wasn't about running a stop sign. *Wow!* I had made the dumbest mistake, and it was too late to correct it. They were already into their search, inside, out, and under. They searched the trunk but never pulled up the mat, leaving them thinking the car was clean.

Suddenly, the lead officer left to answer a dispatch call. Upon his return, the two cops shared a brief conversation and decided to let me go, never issuing a ticket. I was sweating, watching them as they searched everything in the car but the Bible sitting on top of the dashboard that housed my derringer and the drugs—mine and those that belonged to the pastor.

I believed the drugs taken from the pastor's church were the sole purpose of the traffic stop. How they overlooked the Bible, large as it was, only God could explain.

Man, I got-ta cut back on using so much. That could have cost me. Somehow, I had to reframe myself. The real Smooth would have never made such a crucial mistake.

I had moved the gun from my pocket to the Bible while traveling because things had begun to appear safer for me, and I was feeling relaxed. After taking the pastor's cocaine, I placed it in the Bible as well, along with several small fifty-dollar packs of TAC, which fit perfectly in the slot together. Leaving the Bible on the dash was careless. I got lucky, but it did make me think about my constant drug use. I thought now it might be getting out of control, causing me not to think clearly.

Finally, I rolled up on Moke, who was walking home from the corner store. I lowered the window and called out, "Moke!"

"Yeah!"

"Hop in."

He climbed in next to me. He could tell right away I had been seriously aggravated. "Dang! Man, you're sweating. Veins are swelling in your forehead."

"Moke! I got-ta get out-ta here."

"What's wrong with you?"

"Your finest Spartanburg local police just harassed me at the four-way. Claimed I ran a stop sign."

"Did you?"

"Hell naw! You know how I travel."

"Okay, then why would they stop you?"

I was a little jittery and refused to say what I thought was the real reason for them stopping me. "Ion know. I'm pondering that myself."

"Then maybe you should ponder this as well—Bee-Bee received a call from Lilah last week after the gala, and her father has been questioning her about you."

"Where is Bee-Bee?"

"They all rode with my dad to church."

"Darn, I need to holler at her before I get out-ta here. But I'm not sure if I should hang around any longer."

"Maybe you shouldn't because I spoke with Lilah that day, too, and she was very upset."

"Man, I just left Lilah's house. She didn't seem at all upset with me."

"Could it be that she just didn't want to show it?"

"Maybe, but why?"

"All I know is she mentioned her father doesn't want her talking to you anymore because something went down at his church."

"Okay, Moke, but was the church the only place where something was supposed to have happened?"

"Yes, that's the only place she mentioned."

Wow, what relief I felt. That church incident had nothing on the shameful and disrespectful act I'd committed at the pastor's home. But what if someone did see me entering his church? No, they couldn't have! I parked the Monte Carlo well out of range of the church's parking lot, and anyway, no one would have known who I was.

"Hey, did she say what went down at his church?" It wasn't right leading him on like that, but I needed to find out what was going on and how much Pastor Bryant really knew.

"No, she never said, only that something strange happened at her father's church, and he wanted to know where you were staying."

"Did you tell her?"

"No, Bee had already told."

"Damn!" I exclaimed, even though I didn't know if that knowledge would help or hurt my situation. It placed me away from the action of his church, but close maybe to jogging his memory. If he knew I was staying at that hotel, maybe it would register who handed him the handkerchief. That could put me in serious danger. *Heck, maybe I should look at getting out of that hotel. He knows something, and someone has placed my Monte Carlo at his church. But who? And what's their motive? Because there was no activity around his church that evening. And if someone did notice my car, they still wouldn't know who the hell I was. In all actuality, he has no proof that I was at either place. Especially not at the hotel, because the military uniform threw him off completely. He never knew it was me. Not only that, but the pastor also never knew he was being followed.*

Still, considering all the unusual circumstances, Lilah's father seemed somewhat aware, given he instructed her not to talk to me anymore. Then there was the cop's harassment at the four-way, and most of all, my car being searched and torn apart with no valid explanation. *Gee, is it possible someone could have noticed me parking the Monte Carlo up the road behind that old water treatment building? If so, they must have watched as I made my way back down the street and across the parking lot to enter the pastor's church. Man! I must not have been the only one watching him that day. If that's the case, and someone did see me, they could have entered the church after me because I don't remember at all if I locked the damn door once I entered, and I left through the side entrance. Whoever was watching and spotted my vehicle, they must have taken the remainder of the drugs that were left in his safe, then called and reported my vehicle as being in the area. 'Cause what was taken by me wasn't enough for the pastor to jeopardize his career. That's why the darn Bible was never checked—it couldn't hold everything the officers were looking for.*

Now I understood why he was so upset. Hell, I would have been too, but Pastor Bryant should have been more heedful of his actions and pastime activities when around his institution.

"Vincent, do you know where his church is? 'Cause Lilah has already mentioned to her dad that you didn't know."

"Moke, even if I did know, what business could I have at her father's church?"

"How would I know? Maybe that's what he's trying to find out."

"Dang, Moke! What are they expecting me to say? You know me better than anyone."

"Yeah, and that's what I'm afraid of. 'Cause if something has happened and you're involved, then maybe you should leave now. Waiting on Bee-Bee could be risky. Heck! I'll catch up to you later in New York."

"Okay, then don't worry. I'll get the rest of my stuff and check out."

But that's not what I did. Instead, I rented a room at the sleazy motel by the railroad tracks closer to their neighborhood. I wasn't feeling comfortable at the exclusive Franklin Inn anymore.

Moke was right. I should have left. But no, not before figuring this shit out. I had only taken one ounce of the pastor's dope. Things just weren't adding up for me.

***

It was the middle of January, a couple of days after the four-way stop, and I was returning to the elegant hotel where I was still registered under "Lieutenant Goldsby." After stepping out of the elevator and making the left turn, I noticed a gap in my door. I took the chance of slowly opening it, and upon entering the room, I was shocked to discover stuff was thrown everywhere. *No way! Look at this—first the Monte Carlo, and now my room!*

The pastor must have done his research and found information on the most likely places I might be staying. Who else could have sent someone? Nobody in town knew who I was. I understood he didn't want me with his daughter, but to have my room ransacked because of it.

"Humm!" I stood against the door, looking back across the room, realizing I'd have to pay for this mess—television trashed, phone pulled out of socket, mattresses turned upside down, and whatever else they could think to charge me with.

I'm not getting it. One ounce of cocaine missing from his safe. Has to be something I'm missing, but what? Even though my Monte Carlo being seen in the area could be tied to the theft, what I didn't get was the fact that what I took didn't warrant all that was happening.

I put on a fresh uniform and returned downstairs with everything running through my mind. Luckily, I found the hotel manager at the front desk. "Mister! Could I holler at you for a minute?"

We entered the hallway leading to the main lobby, and after we stopped, he said, "Lieutenant Goldsby, may I help you?"

"Yes, I'm curious why my room has been ransacked."

"Officer Goldsby, there is always a significant amount of interest in our Colored guests."

"To the point of destroying a guest's room?"

"No, sir! Absolutely not!"

"Look, do you know the person or persons who could be responsible for this?" I was calmly asking for any clue I could acquire.

"No, I do not, sir, and maybe I shouldn't, but I will say that several days ago, the mayor's assistant did question our guest registration list. But your name did not appear to be one in question."

"Why would the mayor's office be interested in your hotel guest list?"

"It was the mayor's office, sir. I didn't ask."

I understood and acknowledged that he really didn't have to tell me anything, but I decided I'd stay in town a couple more days. I needed to figure things out.

"Hey, I didn't get your name."

"Orlando, sir."

At that point, I ripped off a piece of paper from a tablet sitting on a desk in the hallway. "Look, take this number. If you hear anything, please give me a call. And before I leave, is there a rental car service in the area?" *I got-ta get out of this Monte Carlo.*

"Yes, sir. West Gate Crossing will be your best choice, off Blackstock Road near Spartan Boulevard."

"Thanks, Orlando. You've been incredibly helpful."

To keep them confused, I'd go back to the dump of a motel on the other end of town. Someone ordered this hit and more than likely paid to have the room ripped apart. The pastor and Moke's dad were the only two with a hint that I could have registered there, and that was only because of the information Lilah had received a few days ago.

Without a doubt, the fake ID and phony registration under Lieutenant Goldsby's name had everyone thrown off. Bee-Bee, Lilah, and their families were the only ones who knew exactly what I looked like. Now that it was understood Lt. Goldsby had been identified as the occupant of that room, not Vincent, the search would have to continue for my whereabouts someplace else. With that knowledge, I would take the opportunity to visit the mayor's office. There had to be a reason that registration list was important to them.

The Army uniform carried a lot of clout, and I figured getting a chance to speak with the mayor shouldn't be a problem. What would be a problem was if the assistant were to notice Officer Goldsby in the military uniform? That would surely put the mayor's assistant into a frenzy, especially after just visiting the hotel and noticing Officer Goldsby's name on its registration list. For Goldsby to suddenly show up would definitely be unusual. That wouldn't stop me from looking around, though.

I continued back to the sleazy motel, not expecting to be followed. After parking on the back side of the motel's parking lot, I dashed inside, stopping at the rear door to look around still missing that someone had followed me. There wasn't anyone in sight, and I calmly continued to my room.

The next morning, I checked on the Monte Carlo, and everything still looked normal. I left it at the rear of the motel. I then proceeded to the front of the building.

It was a typical brisk January morning. "Taxi!" I called, capped with a loud whistle.

"Where to?"

"West Gate Crossing. The rental car service."

All West Gate had available was a dark-colored AMC Pacer. It wasn't the prettiest ride, but it served the purpose. I told them thanks for the kind service and left for the city hall. After arriving and parking on the side of the building, it was just a short walk to the front entrance.

"Miss, is the mayor in, please?" I asked the clerk.

"Do you have an appointment, sir?"

"No, I wasn't told one would be needed. I'm on a special assignment from the Army Reserve and was ordered to reach out to him." That was the only thing I could think of at the moment, and I wasn't sure what would happen next. I really didn't care to speak with him. I was there for his assistant.

"It's nine o'clock, so he's in his Wednesday morning meeting, sir. Have a seat. I'll get someone to assist you."

I sat just long enough for the receptionist to be distracted. When that happened, I stood up, entered the corridor of the building, and waited until a man showed up at the clerk's desk. She pointed to where I'd been sitting, and when he turned to look, I saw it was him, the same guy I'd seen with the pastor in the lobby of the Franklin Hotel. Could this be the same person who'd checked the hotel registry guest list? It was someone from the mayor's office, the hotel manager had explained.

If he and the pastor were working together, it would make sense that the mayor's office would take an interest in the hotel registry, especially if someone had reported seeing the Monte Carlo near the church and a link was made between me and the theft. Still, I may have initiated the problem, but only as a gesture to warn the pastor of his wrongdoings. *Something else went wrong. This is too much for an ounce of cocaine and a handful of weed.*

I had to find out what the hell else had happened at his church and how deep they were into their drug connection. I was also beginning to wonder who else was involved. Did Moke's dad have a part in this mess?

I managed to vanish from the city hall without being noticed. Luckily, there was a phone booth on the corner. I needed to speak with Bee-Bee.

"Smooth, is this you?"

"Yeah, I need to holler at you. Can you get free?"

"I think so."

"Can we meet at the corner store down from your house?"

"Sure. Give me about ten minutes. Can you do that?"

"Yeah, you got it. I'm leaving now and headed your way. I should be there in about fifteen."

I pulled close to the curb, where I found her standing next to a parking meter. Damn, she was fine, standing at about five foot seven, her backside stacked like an Olympic sprinter.

"Smooth! Whose car is this?"

"Get in, Bee."

"Where're we headed?" she asked after entering the car.

"Somewhere we can talk in private. Just relax." With that, she seemed inclined to trust me. She sat back and propped her feet up on the dashboard. Bee was a little quicker and more of a hood rat than her friend.

"Why're we here? Why you bring me to a motel? No, Vincent, we can't."

"Calm down, Bee-Bee. It's not what you think. I just need some privacy. Come with me."

Once we entered the room, she seemed stunned. "Man, Moke told me you were registered on the other side of town. Have you been at this place all along?"

"Come on, Bee. Let's not worry about that. Here, have a seat on the bed and just update me on what you know, even what Lilah knows."

"First off, everybody is implying to Lilah's father, your car was seen parked at or around his church. Did you do something at her father's church?"

"Is that what they're saying? What happened at his church? Do you know?"

"No, but Lilah's father told her to stay away from you. He's tried keeping her away from guys before, but it's different this time. After church service the other day, Daddy was scolding Moke Jr. about you, and it seemed serious. Apparently, he wasn't getting anything out of him, and Daddy stormed out of the house. I've never seen my dad so irate. He almost slung the screen door off the hinges. Could my brother be involved in something? If so, you need to tell me. Daddy's a cop. He's going to find out."

"No! Bee-Bee, relax. Your brother is the closest thing to a saint, and he would never do anything wrong." I wanted to console her, and as for me, nobody had mentioned anything yet about what actually happened, and I was going to stay closed shut about it.

Chapter 7. Unannounced Visit

Clack-clack. The door striker was loud and startled us.

"Who's there?" I asked.

"It's the police!"

"Vincent, why would the police be here?"

"I don't know..." I could tell she was scared by the way she jumped from the bed and stood behind me.

"It's Officer Crain with the county sheriff's office!" he said outrageously loudly. "Open up!" I proceeded to open the door, standing, and watching as one of two officers stepped in and walked rapidly past me.

"You stand right there!" he ordered, totally locked in on Bee-Bee. In the same profoundly loud voice, he asked, "What in the hell are you doing here?"

But before I could hear her answer, I was out cold with a blow to my temple.

In a later conversation, Bee-Bee explained exactly what happened, illustrating how, while Officer Crain was about to grab and remove her safely from the room, Officer Frank from the city precinct, whom everyone called "Big Frank," snuck up and landed the blow. She knew I had been seriously hurt, and Officer Crain must have too, because he ordered Frank to inform the desk clerk that an emergency vehicle was needed immediately. She said Big Frank was cocky and walked with a smile on his face to address the clerk as if his mission had been accomplished.

My eyes had just opened when I heard a familiar loud voice. "Finally, you're awake!" Officer Crain said while standing over me.

"What day is it?" I asked.

"Thursday, near noon January twentieth."

"Dang! You mean I've been out for nearly twenty-four hours? Where's Bee-Bee, and what the fuck happened?" I looked around, realizing it was a hospital room.

"Officer Frank unintentionally struck you. Don't worry, though, the doctor has pronounced you'll be okay."

"I don't feel like I'm okay, and who in the heck is Officer Frank?"

"Look, young man, we've experienced a lot of disturbances since you've been here, and we need answers." Officer Crain had been assigned to my hospital room to be the first to question me once I awakened. "What can you tell me about Pastor Bryant's church? I'm told you were spotted in that area last week when the church was entered illegally."

"I don't know anything about no church, and what does any of that have to do with your officer hitting me?" Everything was a bit confusing to me while lying there, especially the part about being knocked out. "Sir, were you told by anyone that I was seen in his church, and what's supposed to have happened at the church, anyway?"

"Son, I'm asking the questions," he said calmly. "What were you doing, and why were you in that area?"

"Officer Crain, is it?"

"Yes."

"You claim I've been a nuisance since my arrival. If so, what have I actually done?"

"Good question, Vincent!" Sergeant Moke entered the room and stood next to my bed. "My apology for Officer Frank. He shouldn't have struck you."

"Why did he, sir? Does he work for you?"

"No! Officer Frank works for the city. As of now, there hasn't been a reason given for his actions. Actually, no city officer should have been dispatched to the area. Of course, if the officer assigned to watch you had done his job, none of this would have happened because we would've known my daughter would be with you."

"Who all was aware of that assignment? Because if the city officer who struck me wasn't supposed to be there, then how do you think he found out?"

Speaking to my best friend's father wasn't like talking to a regular cop. He seemed to have more concern about my welfare and well-being. However, my asking such an official question, he seemed to be quite flustered and reluctant to answer.

"Only Deputy Crain and the pastor, who I trust, knew I was sending someone up to that room," he finally answered.

"So, if you didn't have me knocked out, then who did?"

"Truthfully, I don't know, but I'm ninety-nine percent positive Officer Frank does, and once I catch up to him, I promise we'll get to the bottom of this."

"Sir..."

"Vincent, relax. Your scar is beginning to bleed."

"But, sir, I got-ta get going. I don't feel safe here. Listening to you, and not to be disrespectful, but Pastor Bryant... that dude is not your friend."

I spoke with a painful-looking frown on my face, my words barely garbled out as if the blow to my temple had left me with a mild case of aphasia. Still, even if the muttering of my words convinced him I'd been hurt, he still didn't like what I had to say.

"You should respect the pastor!" he shouted down at me. "Why would you say he's not my friend?"

"Because, Sergeant Moke, there's a certain relationship that's puzzling me I was hoping you could shed some light on."

"Okay, Vincent, but what significance would this relationship have on our conversation?"

"Everything! How well do you know the mayor's assistant?"

"I don't know his assistant personally, only as a member of the city's official staff."

"Sir, have you ever been able to place the two of them together? The mayor's assistant and the pastor?"

"Vincent, what the heck does any of this have to do with the pastor or his church?"

"Look, Sergeant Moke, again—I got-ta get going. There's something I should tell you, but first, you got-ta make sure I get out of this place. Once I'm gone, I'll see to it you receive the information. But I can't, and I repeat, *can't* tell you everything, but I will share what I can with you."

"How do I know you can be trusted?"

"You don't, sir, but what do you have to lose? And I promise you will thank me." By now, I could barely move my head, which was swollen and throbbing. Still, I continued to probe. "Oh, and one other thing, Sergeant—how did you find out about the sleazy motel?"

"Son, after agreeing with the pastor to have the room you supposedly occupied searched, we found it empty and basically unused, which was surprising. However, some small wrinkles in the bed were a sign that someone may have been using it. Afterward, an officer was assigned to follow anyone who paid that room a visit. When you showed, we had you followed, and you led the officer directly to the motel where you were actually staying, only to give him the slip while he watched the Mote Carlo from the rear. That's why we didn't know my daughter would be with you.

"Sir! Than it was you, who had the room ransacked."

"No! The room shouldn't have been ransacked, only searched for any clue to verify your occupancy."

"Vincent, here's my number. When the doctor signs your release, give me a call, and I'll send someone to get you. You must be careful once you're released. I've never seen the pastor so unsettled that he asked for my personal and professional help. I'm not sure if there wasn't anything else that went wrong, but what I'm aware of is more than enough. The church's side window was broken, and a significant amount of cash, jewelry, and municipal bonds were reported missing from a safe. I have to get to the house, but son, you get some rest, and I'll see you soon."

I lay there motionless, thinking, *What the heck?* This was one crooked-ass pastor, and I didn't see any of that stuff in his safe.

***

"How is he, Daddy?" Bee-Bee asked after he entered the kitchen.

"He'll be fine. His head is wrapped, and he'll have a lump for a little while, but he's all right. He did ask for you when he opened his eyes."

"Is it all right to visit him?"

"Yes, but take Moke Jr. with you, and Bee-Bee—whenever you go, make sure Lilah isn't with you."

"Daddy, she's my friend."

"That's why I'm asking you to stay away, at least until I get to the bottom of this squabble. Just promise me you'll stay clear of Lilah until this church quarrel is settled."

"All right. I promise."

"Good, because something is seriously wrong, and Moke, your friend—I believe he has the answers I need. You guys can visit, but Moke, see to it that your sister is all right while you all are visiting him."

"Okay, Daddy, but you know how Bee-Bee is."

Officer Crain was assigned to watch them and to inform Sergeant Moke of any city officers who were seen in and around the hospital. The pastor was considered a true and longtime friend. I, on the other hand, was someone he barely knew. My gut feeling was he was probably wondering why he should trust this kid over someone so prominent who was considered invaluable to this community. Maybe he didn't trust me, but he did consider looking into Pastor Bryant's dealings with the mayor's assistant. He pulled someone from the force he knew could help in achieving his goal.

"Sir, you wanted to see me?" Detective Pleasant asked as he entered Sergeant Moke's office. Moke knew Pleasant had at one time worked for the city, and closely with the mayor himself. He was very detailed and super sharp, the best investigator on the force. From my understanding, Pleasant was assertive but also loyal—ready and willing to do whatever was asked of him.

"Yeah, come in. Close the door. I need to speak with you about Chatman, the mayor's assistant. Have a seat,"

"I would rather stand, sir. What is it you need to know about Chatman?"

"What can you tell me about him?"

"Well, sir, to me he's not a very good guy, and as I see it, he shouldn't have the damn job."

"Continue."

Detective Pleasant bit his lip and continued courageously, "He's an educated thug who hides behind his degree and will do anything to get ahead."

"How do you know this?"

"We came up together, and he happens to be my frat brother. It's a shame, having to honor him. He's always been out for a quick hustle."

"Well, Pleasant, I need you to find out whatever you can on him in the next twenty-four hours."

"Don't worry, Sergeant. I'll have what you need in a few hours."

***

"Daddy, he's gone!" Bee-Bee screamed through the phone after Detective Pleasant had left the office.

"Who's gone?"

"Vincent! The medical clerk said the doctor was holding him through the weekend for observation and couldn't sign his release form until Monday. But when we walked into his room, he wasn't there!"

Chapter 8. Getting Even

"Can I get you anything?" the waitress asked.

"A hot chocolate. Do you have any?"

"Sure. Coming right up."

It was a Friday morning in January after I had discharged myself early from the hospital and made my way back to the motel to retrieve the rental and my black carrying pouch. Soon after entering the room, I noticed after quickly removing the nightstand beside the bed, the pouch was gone.

"*Fuck!*" I screamed out... Who the heck could have grabbed it. Now, how will I be able to pay for the school? About as mad as a person could be, I drove myself to a small restaurant downtown, close to the city precinct where I figured this Officer Frank could be found. I wasn't one who believed in a quick retaliation, but this dude had crossed the line. He had to pay, but first I had to find out what he looked like, then where he lived.

I noticed a big sign posted by the door: "Police officers on duty eat free." *I guess they're rewarded for knocking people out with no solid evidence of any wrongdoing.*

"One hot chocolate. Is there anything else, sir? By the way, you don't look too well. Are you all right?"

"No, I was in a car accident."

"I'm so sorry!"

"And I was told by an Officer Frank that my accident report could be picked up at the precinct down the street."

"Good luck with that."

"Why, do you know him?"

"Yeah, everybody knows Big Frank. Anything else I can help you with?"

"Yes, this officer you called Big Frank—do he and the others eat here?"

"No, usually not. Most go to Cosatu's restaurant two blocks up the street. You'll find him and his partner there around eleven." She walked away, looking back with a weird expression. I went to pay for my cocoa, but before leaving, I handed her a sizable tip and asked, "Would you happen to know Officer Frank's last name? And maybe you could give me a brief description of what he looks like. It would give me a general idea as to whom I'm approaching."

"You must not be from here."

"Why's that?"

"Because you'd know what Big Frank looks like, and for sure you'd know he's a Cosatu. But don't worry, his hat is as big as his ego. You'll know who he is when you see him."

After receiving his full name and a small description, I entered a phone booth sitting in the corner of the restaurant, hopeful of finding an address for Officer Frank. I owed this bastard, and then I'd get the hell out of his town.

Shit, there it is! Frank Cosatu.

I ripped the page out of the book and left, but not before giving the waitress a nod on my way out and picking up a *Spartanburg Herald.*

Once settled into the rental car, I turned the ignition, left the restaurant, pulled up the street just a little ways past Cosatu's, and waited for Officer Frank and his partner to arrive. *Heck, at least this way I can see what the fellow who knocked me the fuck out looks like.*

From where I parked, the main window to the restaurant was in view, making where I was sitting suitable to observe everything going on inside. While periodically surveying my surroundings, I scanned through the *Herald* as well. That made the time seem to move along quite rapidly.

The restaurant had begun to fill with all types of business associates, pulling off their scarves as they came in to get warm with a hot cup of coffee and an early lunch. Several police officers were there, but I couldn't tell if Big Frank was one of them without getting closer. While exiting the car, I noticed the mayor's assistant show up and approach a table. All of a sudden, one of the officers sitting there stood up and removed himself. The mayor's assistant took his seat next to the remaining officer, a really huge fellow, and struck up a conversation. I took it this oversized person was probably Officer Frank.

The unfolding of this event made it imperative I get inside and find a way of getting close to their table, though this large scar on my temple could be a problem, especially if the officer happened to be Big Frank. He was bound to get suspicious seeing the only Colored person in the restaurant, and one with a knot as big as a damn golf ball.

To cut down on any attention, I thought hiding the scar would be wise. That would give me the flexibility to move around. With that thought, it dawned on me I had passed a thrift store on the way here. I exited the rental car and started to walk in that direction. It was better than two blocks, but it was worth the walk. Upon entering the store, I decided on a skullcap, perfect for what I needed to hide my bruise.

Sometimes in life, even without a plan, you have to take a chance. Officer Frank, or Big Frank as most seemed to address him, had only seen me once, and that was lying face down on the floor. Whether or not he got a good look, I don't know, but this was a chance I was willing to take. Hell, I'd always been told we're all supposed to look alike, anyway.

I returned to the restaurant, determined to get as close to his table as possible. That actually went better than expected, and I approached virtually undetected, especially after the purchase of my black winter beanie, which gave me the look of a young Marvin Gaye. That provided a golden opportunity to sit at the corner of the bar on the stool closest to their table.

The mayor's assistant did not stay long after I returned from the thrift store—just enough to sip his coffee, say a few hushed words, and pass an envelope to the officer. It was probably a payment for services rendered—knocking me the heck out. But there was no way for me to really know. I was sitting close, but not close enough to hear the core of their conversation.

Once they stood up, the mayor's assistant spoke again, this time several decibels higher. He said in a high-pitched voice, "Officer Cosatu, it's been a pleasure doing business with you again, and you take care of yourself."

I was also now able to read the officer's badge, which read: *Cosatu, F.*

Satisfied at getting a good look at my attacker, I left the restaurant determined to find his house, just to give myself a general overview of how his neighborhood looked and see what could be done to this dude. I also wanted to know if there was any possible way to enter his home without getting caught. I sure didn't want to show up at his house later that night and be confused about what I should do. Hell, it was early, only a little after 1 p.m. I had plenty of time. After finding his place, I could scan his house plus the area I would need to park the rental.

Once I arrived at his home, the very first thing I saw was a beautiful Chrysler Imperial, a two-door convertible sedan, sitting in his driveway. Accomplishing what I had in mind seemed to be a simple task, nothing too complicated to achieve, definitely not for me.

After doing as much research on the premises as needed, I returned to the thrift store to purchase specific items needed to complete my task. After finishing my little shopping spree, I headed back over to the Franklin Hotel, where I was still registered under Officer Goldsby. No one knew who he was other than the hotel desk clerks and their manager. My body was weak, my head was pounding, and I needed some rest. Still, with the amount of anger that had built up in me, I could barely wait until dark. *And I don't give a damn if he's at his house 'cause I owe this dude.*

Anita the desk clerk, and I made eye contact as soon as I opened the door to the lobby. After checking in with her and finding out there had been no inquiries or further issues concerning my stay, I was informed that management had agreed to pay all damages caused by the mayor's office and was willing to offer me a different room and a better location for the rest of my visit. Finally getting to bed after receiving such a lovely gift must have truly relaxed me because I fell right asleep.

Once I awoke several hours later, it occurred to me it was about time. I quickly got dressed, headed downstairs, and hopped into the rental. Before taking off, I spread out over the Bible some of the pastor's cocaine mixed with a little of the potent TAC I had been keeping in one of my velvet sports jackets. I shaped several parallel lines and then pulled one after the other.

Snorting that much the way I did would give any man an enormous amount of bravery. With that extra moxie, I drove down Main Street, watching as the lights got brighter, changing into different spectrums of color. Obviously, this was caused by the chemicals that I had just consumed. I enjoyed the mixture of the two drugs while listening to James Brown sing one of my favorite songs, "The Payback." The drugs were powerful, though, and I still had to keep a clear head.

After parking up the street away from his house and observing how dark it was, I grabbed my gear and walked back along the road, staying close to the curb. However, the streets all around looked to be completely empty, I continued, one foot in front of the other, refusing to walk the sidewalk until I was closer to his house, mostly to avoid upsetting any neighborhood dogs.

Soon, their narrow walkway became visible. A sharp right and a short walk led me up to his house. I didn't see his car anymore. He must have parked it inside. The driveway sloped down to the garage, which must have been adjacent to a basement. Trying not to disturb anyone, I took another right, walked around back, and found a basement window.

From my toolkit, I took a new glass cutter and a miniature suction cup. Placing the suction cup to the center of the glass to be cut first. Quietly, I cut a full square out of the window frame and attached its handle. Holding the small handle of the suction cup, I removed the glass and began to crawl through.

There was no light in the basement, so it was completely dark inside. After crawling headfirst through the window, I knocked over a flowerpot sitting on a file cabinet.

"Mommy!" said a child's voice close to the basement stairs. "What's that noise?"

"Frankie, baby," a woman answered, maybe Big Frank's wife, "you stay right here. Mommy will check. I hope nothing's fallen and broken."

She opened the door and turned on a dim light while taking several steps down into the basement. Suddenly, something ran from behind the deep freezer and up the stairs. Startled, she turned and followed the creature up, neglecting to turn the light off.

"See, sweetie? It's only One-eyed Sarah. Your cat must have knocked something over. Don't worry, we'll clean up whatever it is in the morning."

I opened the door leading to the garage and found Big Frank's Imperial. I opened a half-gallon bottle of solvent purchased from the hardware store and poured half over the outside of the car. I then poured enough into the gas tank to do the trick, and the rest I dumped onto the upholstery.

Within a few weeks, the surfaces of the car would be destroyed by the solvent, the interior completely shredded into rags and the exterior paint peeled to bare metal. The solvent in the system would only make the car smoke until the gas tank was completely drained. By the time Officer Frank figured out what had happened to his car, his headache would be as bad as the one he had given me. The next time he agreed to knock someone out, maybe a thought process would take place first. I continued to look around only for a few minutes, hoping Big Frank had taken my pouch and decided to hide it someplace down here. The pouch carried nearly eight thousand dollars. Cash I'd planned to use for school. Nonetheless, if it were taken by him, time was a factor, and I couldn't continue to look.

***

Using that same filing cabinet to stand on, I climbed out the basement window without drawing further attention. Once out of the basement, the walk back to the vehicle wasn't nearly as petrifying.

I returned to the sleazy motel and hurried inside to call Bee-Bee before going upstairs to get the rest of my stuff.

"Man, are you okay? My dad has several people out looking for you. We thought something happened!"

"I'm good, Bee, but I need your help."

"Sure, but what can I do?"

"You can tell Moke I'll catch up to him in Brooklyn and remind Lilah of our campus visit in a few weeks."

"Okay, I can do that," she said, neither of us aware yet that Lilah had played me.

"Hey! You remember that rental car we used?"

"Yes, I remember."

"You'll find it at that spot I last saw you. Also, in the glove box is enough cash to keep it for a week. Please see that it gets back. I have got to get out-ta here."

49

"Smooth!" she almost yelled. Then, her voice trembling through the phone, she asked, "When will I see you again?" I think she had begun to care for me like a feisty brother she'd never had.

"Don't worry, Bee-Bee. Just continue your efforts to get into college. When I return in a few weeks, I'll pick you up, and we both can visit Lilah."

I hung up, thinking about Lilah and the pastor. *Damn her daddy!*

Chapter 9. Defeating the Odds

"Could I get this cashed, please?"

I had entered the city of Richmond, Virginia, early Monday morning, way too early to camp out in the bank's parking lot, but I waited there for no other reason than wanting to be first in line. That also gave me the opportunity to watch the employees exit their vehicles one by one to enter the bank for the start of what should've been a normal day of banking. Now I was standing before the teller as she examined the check I'd just laid on her counter.

"Yes, Mr. Lamond! Do you have your driver's license and account number, please?"

"I don't have an account," I said as I handed over my license.

"Well, sir, your driver's license and one other form of ID will work as well."

"It's a Bank of America cashier's check!" I said assertively. "You have my ID. It's valid. Why would I need that other stuff?"

In spite of my tone, she remained friendly. "One moment, sir."

***

I was trying to cash a five-hundred-dollar check I had received from my son's mother, Karol. I'd received it before leaving Oklahoma, she was excited that I was coming to New York and wanted to help out. After returning to the motel from the hospital, the pouch holding all my extra cash was missing. Only what was in my console and in my pockets after I was knocked unconscious was left to travel with. I had to get this cashed, or I'd be stranded.

The supervisor approached the teller booth.

"Mr. Lamond, I'm sorry. If only you had one other form of identification, we would be delighted to help you."

I had arrived early that morning, and I watched everyone, including the supervisor, as they exited their vehicles and headed into work. I didn't know who they were obviously, but I paid close attention to their vehicles and could remember the clothing they were wearing. After my request was denied, I made the decision to follow the supervisor and a coworker to lunch, not knowing exactly what I should do. One thing I did know, though—I needed to gain the supervisor's trust.

As luck would have it, there was limited parking at the shopping center they pulled into, requiring them to park far from the entrance of the food court. I parked close and watched. They had to walk a long way across the parking lot to get there, and they were laughing and talking as they distanced themselves from the car.

My mind was working while I watched, and my eyes monitored them closely until they entered the restaurant. My scheming wasn't going well, but I had to try something. Suddenly, I opened the glove box and found the valve stem wrench I had kept there since installing my gangster whitewalls. I got it out and made my way to their vehicle. Once there, I bent down and screwed a valve stem out of the passenger-side front tire, letting the air out until it was flat. After replacing the stem, I found the right spot to watch for their return. After waiting about thirty minutes, they reappeared, and I made sure to walk by just as they noticed the deflated tire.

"Are you having trouble?"

"Yes! We seem to have a flat."

"Do you have a spare?"

"Sure. I just purchased this car last month. Let me pop the trunk."

Like she said, the vehicle was new, so finding her jack and tire-changing tool wasn't a problem. After replacing the right front wheel, I stood back up, hoping the supervisor would recognize me.

"Wait a minute. Weren't you in the bank earlier this morning?"

"Yes."

"You're the guy with the cashier's check," she said, pointing her index finger at me as she spoke. "Was another bank able to help you with that?"

"Not yet," I answered somewhat pitifully.

"Well, I'm Arline, the branch manager. Since you helped us out, let me help you out. Come back to the branch, and I'll cosign and process that check. There should be more people in the world like you."

"Thanks, Arline! I really appreciate it."

"Of course. And if for some reason I'm not available, Sandra here is our senior teller. She'll be glad to help you."

Honestly, I didn't like what I had just done. It wasn't a good deed, but I needed help, which goes to show—it's not always about rules and regulations, it's about who you know.

I closed her trunk and proceeded to my Monte Carlo. After my little shady and dishonest act, I returned to the bank where everything was handled smoothly. Arline cosigned my check, Sandra the senior teller cashed it, and I was on my way, breathing a sigh of relief. After all of that, I found a place to stop where I could make a call.

"Hello, Natalie speaking."

I hadn't spoken with Natalie for some time, but I wanted to get back in touch. What I felt inside when thinking of her wasn't normal, and she wasn't either. Her personality was distinctive, and she showed a range of qualities as an individual. She was complex in the way she presented herself, and I was amazed by that. She was like no one I'd met, and whatever caused those traits of hers, it was something I wanted to be a part of. I knew from the first day I laid eyes on Natalie that I wanted her in my life. Therefore, whatever it took to accomplish the goal of us being together, my mind was set on making that happen in spite of the "It" that controlled my actions. Whenever it was finished with me, no matter its duration, I would make it happen. The others who were in my life at that time I met Natalie I needed for one reason or another, but it was Natalie I wanted. I was locked in on her.

"How are you?" I asked.

"Fine. Where are you?"

"I'm in the Washington, DC, area, headed to New York. I found a private investigator school to attend. I wanted to let you know. I'll try calling you at least once every other month."

"You promise?"

"Yes. I'll call again in late March."

"Okay, Vincent, and take care of yourself."

***

Afterward, I continued my journey, trying to make it as far north as possible before stopping again. When I did finally pull over in South Jersey, I made a very significant call.

"Karol, please."

"Speaking. Is this Vincent?"

"Yes. It's a little late, but I wanted to let you know I'll be there early tomorrow morning."

"What happened? You had me worried. You were supposed to have been here earlier this month."

"Don't worry. I'm a'ight. Just got a little tangled up. Tell my son I'll see him in the morning."

"No, Vincent. I can't do that."

"Why not? I'm not that far away."

"Because you've disappointed him more than enough. Just call me when you arrive."

***

Finally, I did arrive in Corona, Queens, and after making an extra block around the complex where Karol and my son were living, I found a place to park on the street. It was 2:00 a.m.

"Number and name of the building, please," a security guard demanded as I stood amazed at the entrance to Lefrak City Apartments.

"Building and apartment number, please," the guard asked again.

"Oh! Paris Tower, 505."

He opened the gate and directed me to her building. When I found her door, I knocked quietly so as not to disturb others. I stood directly in front of the door's tiny window and waited.

"Come in," she said in a low tone after opening up. "Why didn't you call, and how did you get here?"

"I'm decent," I said sarcastically after stepping inside.

She locked the door behind us. "Excuse me for that. How are you? I was expecting you to call."

"My apologies, Karol, but traffic was light, and I was feeling pretty good, so I kept driving, and after getting a couple of city and state maps from the service stations, here I am." It wasn't only the maps I stopped for, but also to do a little of the pastor's cocaine and sometimes a line of my own TAC mixed with just a touch of the pastor's weed. It may have been what kept me awake and able to drive so far.

***

When daylight arrived later that Tuesday morning, everyone awoke and was moving around. It was the first time the three of us had been together alone as a family, and our son was old enough to capture the moment and carry it as a memory. I won't lie—it was such a captivating experience, and it was just as exciting to me as it was to him.

After eating breakfast, seeing my son off to school and his mother off to work for the very first time was amazing—both empowering and slightly surreal to digest. I was all smiles as they were leaving, but then came reality. First, the elevator got hung up on the second floor, forcing me to use the emergency equipment to notify maintenance.

The door was soon open, and after making it downstairs to get my stuff out of the Monte Carlo, I found it sitting on blocks. Some bastards had stolen all four wheels. I was standing by the front fender of the car as the street sweeper was passing through. The guy kindly stopped to inform me I had approximately twenty-four hours to have it removed from the street before it would be towed away. Remember, now I was in Corona, and I didn't know a soul other than the two people I had just watched leave the apartment. After filing a theft report with the authorities, it was imperative I find my way to the private investigator school and be on time for my appointment.

Chapter 10. Enrolling in School

"Hey! Smooth!" I heard a loud voice call from the street as the security gate closed behind me. I turned and saw two guys sitting in a vehicle, but how could they know my name? I had on a pair of jeans with the name Smooth pressed on one leg, but neither of them could see it. I continued in stride until reaching the driver's side door of their car.

"Yes! Who are you?" I asked.

"We're a nationwide affiliate that has been given inside information on the performances of former government employees with strong resumes. Vincent, yours is impressive, and we're willing to make you an offer. We understand that time is a factor this morning, so here—take our cards. They have our Yonkers address and phone numbers. We'll be anticipating your call, Vincent, or we'll be seeing you later this evening. At that time, everything will be explained to you."

"Sure." I looked at the card and said, "You guys have a nice day."

Who are they, and how in the hell could they possibly know I'm here in New York? After leaving and continuing with my thoughts, I caught the very next bus to the subway and hopped a train downtown. I was told the school was located on Washington and 4th. Sure enough, I found a marquee that read "Superior Career Academy of Investigations" staring me directly in the face as soon as I emerged from the subway onto the street. A big red arrow pointed toward the school, and I felt slightly nervous and insecure as I beheld the building—one of New York's patented high-rise buildings.

I stood and checked myself, and my confidence surged again after checking the appearance of my clothing. With that, I approached the building.

Before I could reach the administration office door, I heard a call.

"Lamond! Vincent Lamond!"

"Juncos! Juan Juncos! Damn, dude, what are you doing here?" Juncos was a Puerto Rican who worked directly under me at the state identification card (SIC) processing department in Oklahoma.

"I enrolled in school last week. We're all here today signing up for our classes."

"Juncos, you're enrolled in this school?"

"Yeah, bro!"

"Man! What a small world this is."

"What brings you to New York?"

"My son and his mother live in Queens. I did a little research at work, and I found this school."

"Boss, you and me in school together!"

"Juncos, it's nice to see you again, but I have to go. I'll catch up with you later."

Damn, millions of people in this city. How could we end up in the same school? There has to be an explanation. We worked together but never shared any personal information. Could he be with the other two guys who gave me their business cards? Here I go again, getting all paranoid, and usually when that happens, it means something's up. I will not let them affect my work, not this time. Just stay on course and enter the school, finish it, and get the hell out of the city. Other than having a chance to spend valuable time with Karol and my son. Attending school was the only other reason I came to New York.

I turned and opened the door with the large black letters printed on the glass that read "Administration Office." I stepped inside, followed the arrows directing me to personnel, and signed the appointment book. It was January 18, and I couldn't believe it, but I'd made it there on time.

"Mr. Lamond?" a woman's voice called after a few minutes of waiting.

"Yes," I answered.

"Good morning, I'm Ms. Whitley. M. E. Whitley, the admissions officer. How are you, and how can I help you today?"

"Thanks for asking, Ms. Whitley, and I'm okay. I'd like to know the cost of the Advanced Investigation and Security class because it wasn't listed in your regular brochure."

"Mr. Lamond, first, may I ask—what will be your plans and means of financing your enrollment with the school?"

"I haven't decided. The cost of the class is my biggest concern."

"Well, Mr. Lamond, whatever they are, we'll be happy to assist with a student loan or with any other financial plan available to get you started. Although that may take some time, causing a slight delay in your enrollment. But we promise to have you registered, not for this class, but before the next session begins. Please give me a minute, and I'll get the information you need."

Shit! I thought. *Why am I sitting my ass here? Once she returns with the amount of the class, whatever it comes to, I won't have it.* After my recovery from being knocked unconscious by Big Frank and returning to the sleezy hotel, I found my pouch missing. Everything I had of value was in that pouch including the cash for both schools. What was left in my possession was a car, a pistol, and a damn ounce of cocaine that didn't belong to me. *How in the heck am I supposed to pull this off? Plus, if I can't make this living arrangement work with Karol, I'm going to be homeless as well.*

"Mr. Lamond, I'm sorry about the wait. For the advanced session in question, with your processing fees, application fee, and the cost of your class, it all comes to a total of 3,875 dollars, which must be paid before the start of your first session."

"Ms., if I may ask, when does the next session start?"

"Vincent, is it?"

"Yes."

"Well, Vincent, the next class starts with its orientation in exactly two weeks. There's only one available seat left. Should I schedule you?"

"Yes, ma'am!"

"Well, Mr. Lamond, welcome to Superior Career Academy of Investigations. When should I expect a payment for your enrollment? The deadline is this coming Friday, the twenty-first."

"Ms. Whitley, if for some reason I can't get the money, how long does it take for a student loan to process?"

"It varies, but don't worry, we'll work extremely hard to get you in school. There's another session that starts in thirty days from the next orientation day."

"Okay, Ms. Whitley. I'll do my best to have a payment by Friday's deadline."

"Great, Vincent! Orientation is two weeks from today, the first of February."

***

Later that afternoon, I exited the subway in the borough of Queens and caught a bus to the Barbizon School of Modeling and Acting. After exiting the bus somewhere around Queens Boulevard and 63rd, I managed to find my way to the school.

"I'm looking for a Kourtney Lockhart. I was told I could find her here. I'd like to enroll."

"I'm sorry, but you'll need to speak with Mrs. Tyler. She's head of admissions."

"Thank you. Where can I find her?" *Hell, this class can't cost that much*, I thought. Oh, how misinformed I was. After getting a chance to speak with Mrs. Tyler and finding out Barbizon was a prestigious modeling school, around twenty-five hundred per term, I realized I had to come up with a plan, but what the heck could I do? No way I could hustle that much in a week. I had no credit, no money, and no damn job.

Needing a solution, I called my man Zo in Edmond, Oklahoma. Zo and I had partnered together on a few banking schemes, mostly check snatching and cashing. He was always up for a hustle.

"Smooth, what's up with you?"

"Not much. I'm in a little bind."

"Well, that's different. I can't see you in a bind."

"Look, can you come up with a check or two?"

"No, I've been transferred, and plus, you always said it was too dangerous."

"Yes. True words."

"Then why break your word?"

"True, Zo. Something you should never do."

"Yo, Smooth, you always been there for me. What are you up against?"

"Shit, Zo. I need six grand by next week to start school."

"Damn! Man, I feel you. If only I were still in the mail room. Hey, I might have something else you could use, especially if you are willing to take a chance on a damn check-cashing scheme."

"What you got?"

"Listen, Vincent—"

"There you go with that Vincent shit again."

"Yes, but you know whenever I call you that, it's serious. Man, I've got an official government money order machine and thirty blank postal money order forms. What do you think? Can you do anything with them?"

"I'm sure I can. The problem lies in the setup. There's no place to set up shop to print my ID cards. Plus, I'm supposed to start school next Monday," I lied. "Not only that, but I'm living in New York with my son and his mother. Man, I can't jeopardize them by getting into something so suddenly."

"Okay. What if I were to front you with the money you need for school? Then when you finish converting the money orders into cash, we settle in the split."

"Are you serious? That may take a month or so."

"Can you get them cashed?"

"Yes, that's no problem, but planning everything is. What's the face value?"

"Max a grand each, and I understand your damn planning procedures," he joked. "They're absurd."

"All right, Zo. Send everything you've got with the money to this address, and I'll make it happen. When it's done, I'll get back to you."

"Okay! I'll get it shipped right away."

I had to let Karol's brother Will know about the incoming package because there was no way I could have it coming to Karol's address. She definitely didn't need to know I was receiving a postal money order machine. She would pressure me about what it was for.

After fitting the Monte Carlo with new shoes early the next day, I needed a safe place to park it. The street meter fees were too high in New York—that would cost around eight dollars a day, which was out of the equation, though I still had part of the five hundred I'd received from Karol left after replacing the tires and wheels. Along with the hundred I had in the console, there was enough to continue parking on the street for about two weeks. Then there was also the fee for the train fare back and forth to school to consider, and if Zo didn't come through for me, considering pushing school back for another month was out of the question for me.

It was the first time I could remember not being in control.

Later that same evening, after having the wheels and tires replaced, I was in a conversation with Karol, watching as she stood in front of the stove preparing an evening meal with nothing on but a wife beater and a pair of booty shorts.

"Karol, do you think your sister Iola would let me park the Monte Carlo in her parking spot at the apartment where she lives, since she don't have a vehicle? You know, being here in New York, I won't be able to use it very much, and it would cost way too much to continue parking on the street."

"Vincent, don't worry about it," she said as she stepped away from the stove, waving a tablespoon in her hand and speaking energetically. She was beautiful and seemed happy we were all together as a family.

She was very young and cute with her round face, light-brown complexion, and large brown eyes. She was small in stature and had a waistline you could hardly see. She was also very intelligent and well educated, having graduated with a degree in accounting from Grambling State University.

"What-ta you mean don't worry about it?"

"As you were having your tires replaced earlier today, I applied for a parking permit for you. It's thirty dollars a month. Here's your temporary card, but there's a stipulation."

"What kind of stipulation?"

"You'll have to park it on the rooftop of the adjacent building."

"Wow! Karol, what can I say? You're a lifesaver, 'cause it would create one heck of a debt being parked on the street every day."

"You don't have to say anything. It's obvious you don't have the money it would take to park out there anyway, and I don't mind helping."

Man, how could I not value this woman?

Chapter 11. Everything Clouding His Birthday

Things were beginning to settle just a little. Will had received the package from Zo, which provided me with enough cash to start both schools. After crossing the enrollment fees from my list of things to get done, I decided it was time to give Officer Moke that call. It was after 6:00 p.m. on Friday, the twenty-first, and catching him at home would be a little less intense. First, I needed to remove myself from the apartment. I didn't feel comfortable talking to Mr. Moke around Karol and my son. Plus, snorting a sizable line of TAC would speed up the intensity of my thoughts and be helpful in talking to him. There was a public phone downstairs. All I needed was a roll of quarters to make it happen, and those I kept in the car, as well as the drugs. I excused myself from the meal and headed to the elevator.

When the feeling of the TAC had climbed to its high, it was time to make the call.

"Mr. Moke, please."

"Give me a minute,"

"Mrs. Moke!" I asked before she could exit the phone. "Yes!" she said. "This is Vincent, how are you?"

"Doing well, Vincent, how have things been with you?"

"Doing good as well, just wanted to touch base with Mr. Moke."

"No problem, I'll see if he's available."

"Vincent. How can I help you?"

"Sir! Is it okay to talk?"

"Yes. I wasn't sure if you would ever call. It's good to know that you're all right. You okay?"

"Yes, I am, sir."

"Vincent, a lot happened in those two weeks you spent here. Other than Pastor Bryant's church incident, I found out that his vehicle was also burglarized. Later we found that Officer Frank's house was broken into, and his car vandalized. You wouldn't know anything about any of that, would you?"

"I—"

"Didn't think so," he cut me off. "Son, you didn't call to hold a friendly conversation. What can you tell me? Because right before you left, one of our best detectives was placed on this case. Please feel free because whatever you have to offer, I promise, it will be appreciated."

"First, I can tell you that Big Frank, as everyone calls him, and the mayor's assistant are working together."

"Who? Chatman and Officer Frank? How do you know this?"

"I watched while sitting on a barstool in Cosatu's restaurant. The mayor's assistant passed him an envelope, and I doubt that it was government related. Sir, I know you think highly of your friend the pastor, but you should know he and Chatman are connected. I witnessed the two of them together at the Franklin Hotel in the midst of some type of meeting. I've also been informed that they meet there every other month or so. I'm almost positive, sir, that those meetings are drug related. Because when I first saw the pastor that morning, he wasn't carrying anything. When the two of them left the room and exited the building, all of a sudden, he was carrying a briefcase."

"So, you're telling me that the pastor is using drugs?"

"Not only is he using drugs, but he's dealing the stuff as well. I'm telling you the pastor is dealing cocaine. No one purchases that much stash for personal consumption—so much he has to carry it in a briefcase. I'll admit that I may have been wrong for following the pastor and being in that area, but I was only trying to help your friend. He's handling weight, sir, and lots of it."

"What do you have on Officer Frank?"

"Nothing. No more than watching that bastard get paid by the mayor's assistant for knocking my ass out, and I'm almost sure that your friend the pastor had it all set up. The pastor was under the impression I had taken a package of his because someone had spotted my Monte Carlo near his church. That's the reason he convinced you to have my vehicle and room searched. Also, you should pay closer attention to that Chatman guy. The dude is all over the damn place. Oh, and one other thing before I let you go—I have a pack of cigarette papers, some Tops belonging to the pastor. If you'd like, I'll mail them to you. Maybe one of his fingerprints will surface."

"Vincent, how did you get all of this information, and why would the pastor have a pack of rolling papers? Where did you get them?"

"Sir, remember what I said—I'll tell you what I can. Let's put it this way—maybe he uses them to test his product because no one is purchasing that much marijuana not to make a profit. I told you once before that friendship is priceless, and he is your friend. We all veer off sometimes, but Pastor Bryant is getting very careless. Maybe you should have a talk with him. I think he's become a little too comfortable."

"Is that it, son?"

"No, sir. I do have one other thing. Could you give Moke Jr. this number and tell him to call me once he arrives? Will you, please?"

"Hmm," he muttered. "Sure, Vincent. No problem. He should be leaving here on the fourth. I'll definitely give it to him. Oh, and by the way, you should know this..."

"I should know what, sir?"

"Lilah's father is furious now that he's found out his daughter is pregnant."

"Pregnant?"

"Yes. And I would like to congratulate you."

"Congratulate me?"

"Yes. But first, I think it would be appropriate if you were to return and become responsible for what you've done."

"Why, sir? It's highly improbable that she's pregnant by me."

"Son! Her father mentioned just yesterday that he received a bill from the Spartanburg General Hospital emergency room. Among the list of treatments was a verification of Lilah's pregnancy. The pastor is claiming that you're the only person his daughter was involved with."

How can he be so sure? His daughter is in college.

"Sir—"

"Vincent, someone's at my door. I have to go but look—you stay out of trouble and take care of yourself."

My thoughts exactly. "I will, sir."

After hanging up, I decided to give Karol's brother a quick call.

"Yo, Will! You gon' be home for a minute?"

"Yeah."

"Cool. I'll be right over."

I caught the elevator and returned to the apartment. "Karol, while you're finishing everything here, I'm going to take DeVaan over to your brother's house with me."

"That's fine but be careful."

It would take too long on the train to get out to Will's place, so DeVaan and I hopped into the Monte Carlo.

Will was waiting when I pulled up to the curb. "What's going on, Vincent?" he asked as DeVaan followed me out the driver's side door. "Dang, dude! How in the heck did Karol let you get away from her with the kid? Come in, though. You must've been flying to get here so soon. DeVaan, go holler at your aunt. She's in her office. She'll be happy to see you."

"Hey, Will," I said once we were alone. "I was wondering—do you have someplace private I could use to fabricate some ID cards and maybe hide a few things?" Karol's brother was one of the few who knew how devious and manipulative I had become.

"Yeah, but not really private. It's where I keep my German shepherd, so no one goes there. Also, it's where I put your package that just came in."

"Man, I can't work around a barking-ass dog!"

"Do you hear one?"

"No."

The dude was different. At first, I didn't understand his question. Then he unlocked a door to a set of stairs and said, "Come, follow me."

He took me to an unimaginable place. It was like an underground puppy-training center. He had been working with this German shepherd since he was a pup, and he'd just turned two. The dog was so well trained and playful, I couldn't believe my eyes.

"Come." he said to the pup.

After clearly walking him across the basement floor, he then said, "Sit." Sitting him next to a very expensive statue. "Vincent, see if you can make him move. I'll be right back. I got-ta get 'em a little treat. I was a little afraid at first to even touch the puppy, but he looked so friendly that I decided to pet him. I grabbed his collar just to see if I could walk with him as Will did. But the dog never moved, no matter the different gestures I would make towards him, he never even barked. "What do you think now?" Asking once he returned. "He's special" I said. "See! He's well managed, and whatever business you have, you'll have workspace, company, and protection."

It was good having a friend like Will. He would always be there for you. And it was no different when it came time to let me use his basement to print those ID cards. He had a heart of gold and never questioned my work. We returned to his living room. I grabbed DeVaan and headed back to the apartment.

The beginning of the week had arrived. Everybody was back at work, and I had a handful of government money orders that needed to be printed. It was me, the printing machines, and a beautiful German shepherd hard at work deep in a basement. There wasn't much to it now that I had the right equipment to complete the work. Still, given I had so many blanks, it took most of the day to make sure they were all done correctly.

The next morning after returning to thoroughly check my work, it didn't take nearly as long as I'd anticipated. Everything was completed and had turned out exceptionally well. Each ID card was prepped with the proper-sized photo, contained all identifying information, and was heat laminated with a plastic cover. The money orders were printed and stamped with the amount of one thousand dollars on each of them. However, I would have to come up with a strategy on how to get them all cashed. I didn't think that would be a problem because school wasn't going to start until Tuesday the first, leaving me with the remainder of the week to brainstorm how to get that done.

For now, I had to feed the puppy and get the heck out of Will's basement. I hoped I could spend the extra time I had gained with Karol and DeVaan. They should be home by the time I got there, I figured.

After closing down the house, everything was going great until I tried to jump onto I-95, where a motorcycle had flipped on its side on the entry ramp and slid up under a delivery truck. That had the traffic on the ramp shut down.

"Damn it!" I said, realizing there would be an extensive wait for the wreckage to be cleared.

As I sat waiting for that to happen, I had nothing better to do than strategize a plan that would be effective in cashing those money orders. However, the night of the gala crossed my mind as we continued to wait for the bike to be removed from under the truck.

When someone knocked on the door, I had quickly pulled out of Lilah and never climaxed. However, she had become pregnant, leaving everyone in doubt about who the father was, except her father, as Sergeant Moke had explained. I promised myself I'd visit her in a few weeks at school.

Fulfilling that promise couldn't have come at a better time. I had seven sets of ID cards and thirty blank money orders worth a thousand dollars each in my possession, and I had seven states and one District of Columbia to travel through just to see her. Incorporating cashing two of the completed money orders in each state before reaching South Carolina seemed creative to me, and it also seemed very possible. The cashing of the money orders would have to take place within a few days to prevent anyone from catching on, though. I'd start by cashing two money orders before leaving the state of New York, preferably at a post office in the lower Manhattan area on the afternoon of the twenty-seventh. After that, I'd cash two more in New Jersey, and two more in each state thereafter until reaching South Carolina. Assuming most or all of the state banks would be closed over the weekend, my plan was to use a couple of days before the weekend and one day after it to complete the job.

Shit, here we go. The vehicles started to move, and I was on my way.

***

As soon as I walked into the living room of the apartment, Karol called, "Vincent!"

"What's up?" I said, entering the bedroom.

"Hey! It's the twenty-fifth, DeVaan's birthday, and it's almost four o'clock. Could you run to the corner bodega? I need some milk for the cake. Oh, and by the way, pick him up from the playground and take him with you. But don't say anything. I'm trying to keep

70

this a surprise, and don't worry if you forgot. I realize you've been busy and have a lot on your mind."

After making it to the end of our hallway and looking out over the fifth-floor balcony down to the playground, I noticed a much larger kid was holding DeVaan upside down by his ankles.

What the fuck? "Put him down!" I yelled. He must have realized I could be headed downstairs when I no longer appeared on the balcony. Whatever his thought process was, when I reached the playground, he had dropped DeVaan.

"Come with me," I said to my young son, and we attempt to walk around the huge complex to the corner bodega.

"Where we going?"

"Your mother needs some milk for the bread. I got-ta go around the corner to the store."

"But, Dad, why are we going this way? The milk'll be spoiled by the time we get back."

I smiled and giggled at what my little one had said. It was quite hilarious. The kid was only seven years of age. "Do you know a better way?" I asked, never thinking he would actually know one.

"Yes, sir! Uncle Will always takes us through the tunnel. It's a straight shot to the front street with only one turn." He yanked at the bottom of my jacket. "Daddy! Daddy! It comes out next to the German store, right where you're headed."

So, through the tunnel we went, a grown man following a seven-year-old. Rats, mice, and all other types of rodents gathered along the sides of the tunnel, eating whatever someone had dropped or thrown away.

"Good evening, Mr. Oskar."

"Hey, DeVaan! What can I do for you this evening, and who is it you have with you today?" the German man asked my son. At that point, I found out my seven-year-old was a regular.

"This is my dad, sir."

"Pleased to meet you," he said as we reached across the little folding gate connecting the two counters together to shake hands.

"My name is Vincent. What's cooking, Oskar?"

"I'm known to the neighborhood as Mr. Oskar," he corrected. "You have a very good kid on your hands. He's going to be something one day."

"Thank you, sir! He does seem to be a pretty good kid."

DeVaan came from around the aisle with his Laffy Taffy and Bubblicious bubble gum and placed it on the counter.

"Is that it, DeVaan?" Mr. Oskar asked. The kid proceeded to peek up over the counter, reaching for his weekly store allowance tablet. I could only stand back and look—a seven-year-old with a store tab.

After paying for the milk along with a dozen eggs, we returned to the apartment. Not in that big of a hurry, we decided not to return through the tunnel. Before reaching the security gate to the apartment complex, the thought of the larger kid holding my son upside down was a concern.

"DeVaan," I said a bit aggressively, noticing a bus stop bench a few feet a head of us, "have a seat. Listen closely, and don't lie to me. Why did that kid have you held in that position? It wasn't safe, and he didn't look to be playing with you."

He looked down, abashed.

"Hold your head up, and don't lie."

Seeming very reluctant and afraid, he began to speak. "He was selling Star Trek walkie-talkies. He let me get two of them, and I never paid him!"

"Darn! How did you intend to pay him? You're only seven years old." I could only wonder if the "It" wasn't only affecting me, but also my son. I decided to keep his little credit account, his secret passageway to the store, and most of all his hustle concerning the walkie-talkies between the two of us. This was something her own brother had not spoken to her about. The last thing I needed was to cause a conflict among us.

Chapter 12. Lilah's Visit

Thursday came fast. I had decided to take a half day and then a full day on Friday to travel. Getting to South Carolina was very important to me, as there seemed no better way to find out about Lilah's situation, and there was definitely no other way to get those money orders cashed so quickly. The money orders didn't bother me as much as Lilah being pregnant did. With the thought of that continuously strolling across my mind, I left.

When I arrived in the state of South Carolina, I was high, really high-high on the TAC I hit before my stop at every bank, especially the ones that had a drive-through window. Sometimes, depending on how I felt, I'd cash both money orders at the same drive-through. Heck, it all seemed legit to me.

It was late Friday evening on January 28 when I saw the school's marquee that read "South Carolina State" with all the beautiful roses and other flowers planted around it and flags flying high above. I had been traveling since noon the day before, and I was excited. I hurried to where I could make a call.

"Hello?"

"Lilah, please," I asked, holding the receiver with a smile and the utmost feeling of joy that I was having a baby. Even if I didn't see how that could be possible, there was still a slim chance that something could have happened. Of course, I wasn't there to see my first child grow from a baby. However, if I created another, it would give me the opportunity to redeem myself.

"This is Lilah. Who am I speaking with?"

"This is Vincent. I'm here at South Carolina State. How are you?" I was as upbeat as a future father could be but hearing the way she barked through the opposite end of the receiver, I was convinced she wasn't carrying the same type of enthusiasm.

"Why are you here?"

"What? You don't remember me promising to visit you in a few weeks?" She acted as if she had fallen and bumped her head, ending up with a case of amnesia.

"Yes!" she said in a doleful voice, "but you were only passing through. I wasn't expecting to ever see you again."

"Hey, is there someplace we could meet?"

"No, I'm on my way to a debate contest."

"When are you returning? Can we talk?"

"There's no reason for us to have a conversation. We have nothing in common, and we're from two different walks of life. There will never be anything between us."

"Shit!" She spoke as if she weren't pregnant at all, and especially not with a child of mine. "But aren't we having a baby?"

"*I'm* having a baby, not you, and I wouldn't want my child raised with two fathers."

"*What?* What the fuck do you mean?" I asked, but to this day, she's never answered.

"Listen, I have to go, but next time, call before you decide to visit."

That evening I was left holding a phone, standing in shock and not understanding what the hell just happened. She never told me if the baby was or wasn't mine. Her statement was, "*I'm* having a baby, not you," and it was left at that.

I hung up, confused, angry, and frustrated. A feeling of love and warmth turned into coldhearted hatred. But I couldn't let that interfere with the work I had left ahead of me, nor could I let it alter my plans. Like she said, we were from two different walks of life. I truly understood, and I wanted to be like all other individuals, but it seemed as though my family history would always come back to haunt me, no matter where I was. It left me thinking I would never be normal, like I was being punished for all the wrongs my father had done.

After what I'd just experienced, leaving Bulldog Country wasn't a problem. Even though the trip itself and the cashing of the money orders had gone well, the call with Lilah was one to be forgotten. Thinking back, I'd promised Bee-Bee we would both visit Lilah. When I returned, though, everything had changed. Bee-Bee was finally in junior college and couldn't make the trip. Not only that, but she and her best friend were not communicating at the time, especially after Bee-Bee found out from her dad that her best friend had lied and kept a secret from her. She knew Lilah better than anyone and noticed she wasn't herself that night at the New Year's Eve party. She also knew that she had never been interested in any man the way she was with me that night. I found out years later from Bee-Bee that Lilah had simply wanted to protect the professor by scapegoating me. She knew her father hated me and would never want me around his grandchild, so blaming me for the pregnancy was the perfect solution. After realizing she didn't care to talk with me, I grabbed a hotel room and waited, but nothing ever happened, she really didn't care to meet with me. I had to gather myself and prepare for the long return journey to New York. I couldn't let all of what had just happened get in the way of my work. I'd go through the same routine heading back, cashing two of the money orders before leaving South Carolina, and two more in each state until there weren't any left.

Chapter 13. Nervous Adventure

As I'd hoped, the return to the city went well, and everything worked as planned. I even visited my former stomping grounds in Cherry Hill, New Jersey. While there, I sat in the Monte Carlo smoking some of the pastor's good weed, a joint I'd laced with a little of his highly impressive uncut cocaine. At some point, the weed started to work. My mind began to wander until it stepped outside its box.

Heck, dude, you could cover three cities in three different states within a seventy-mile radius while in this area.

Yes, the marijuana was working! My wandering mind was in a new state of consciousness. It was truly open. I could cover the tri-state area of Pennsylvania, Delaware, and New Jersey within a couple of hours, leaving only four remaining money orders to be cashed before reaching New York.

Frustrated as I was leaving South Carolina, I couldn't think of anything better than cashing two of the remaining money orders in Washington, DC. At that particular time, I was vexed, and those two appeared special to me. Cashing them at a Bank of America in our nation's capital just seemed appropriate. Traveling north on Pennsylvania Avenue, the light turned red. As I stopped, I looked through the passenger-side window. There it was—the Bank of America building, the largest banking institution in the US, staring me right in the face.

After parking and stepping out of the car, I stood there aghast, looking up at the bank. It wasn't nearly as large as I had mentally pictured, but the beauty of its architecture had me so dazed and amazed that I could only stand and stare. None of that made me uneasy, though, not the beauty of its structure or even the size of the building. Actually, it was the credibility of its name, Bank of America, that troubled me.

As I started to prep myself, I looked down at my watch and realized it was early—7:48 a.m. I couldn't enter yet. I had completely lost track of time. I also realized it was almost time for the Petey Greene show. After returning to the Monte Carlo, I found a breakfast house and took in a light meal, then located the nearest hotel. Heck, no one would be keeping track of who spent the night there. Therefore, I could sit, relax, and watch *Petey Greene's Washington* in peace. I was seriously startled by how that guy could bring people together with just the sound of his voice. There was something special about that dude, especially the way he could say something, anything, and make it seem acceptable.

As Petey Greene's talk show was about to reach its conclusion, my thoughts were beginning to focus on the bank all over again. Even though the remarkable TV show had me energized, my own thoughts were causing my premature defeat. Just the name "Bank of America" had me doubting myself, and that was something I'd never done. One couldn't help but be inspired after watching a Black man with his own TV show, and that I was. So, my mind clicked. I left the hotel for the Monte Carlo, retrieved my bag, and quickly returned to one of their large and elegant restrooms. Officer Goldsby's uniform was still freshly cleaned, and it was a superb disguise. I'd used six of the previous seven Id's already, and considering this Id matched with a special military uniform, could offer what you would consider confidence and courage. I knew of no one who wouldn't give an officer their due respect.

After changing into Officer Goldsby who had not appeared since Spartanburg, I noticed that all of my nervous tendencies had calmed to a minimum. As I approached the bank, though, seeing the all-glass front door with the FDIC logo and the corridor beyond was a bit much for me. It had my palms sweating, my stomach fluttering, and my heart palpitating like a bass drum. But none of that mattered. I had already successfully cashed money orders in seven states, collecting over twenty-six thousand dollars in the span of a few days. Plus, I had every piece of information on Officer Goldsby that I needed, and that uniform gave me the illusion of legitimacy." Respecting our nation's capital and accepting that they had some of the most high-powered surveillance and best special service agents in the world, I understood the challenge ahead would be difficult, and that was something I loved. Even though I understood the odds and disadvantages I was working with, I never gave it a thought that anyone would catch me.

I entered the bank and found it much less busy than I'd expected. I surveyed the perimeter inside the bank and noticed the only cop was sitting relaxed, reading a pamphlet, and for the most part not paying attention to anything going on around him. This was all surprising to me.

I then set my eyes to finding whoever looked to be the oldest teller. I loved making them smile and feel as though they were super important. Not only that, but a veteran teller would rarely have to ask for assistance, as they would have experienced most unusual transactions. After choosing one, I approached "Josie," as it read on her name tag, not smiling this time but with tears slowly forming in my eyes.

"May I help you, sir?" the elderly teller asked.

"Ms. Josie, how are you this morning?"

"Wonderful, thank you for asking, but are you all right?" she inquired with what seemed to be a deep concern for me.

"Yes," I said while searching for a handkerchief to wipe my eyes, one I knew all along I didn't have.

"Here, sir, take this..." She handed me a tissue pulled from the box sitting to her left. "What can I do for you this morning?"

I laid the two money orders on the counter. "I'd like to get these cashed, please, if it's possible."

"Sure, let me have a look," she said, picking them up from the counter. "Are you sure you're all right, sir?" she asked as if she meant it from her heart.

"My uncle was ill and passed away. I'm doing my best to help with his funeral arrangements. I had planned to mail those, but suddenly I was told it was too late. After hearing that, I decided to bring them along with me."

"Here!" She slid the box of tissue closer to me and looked directly at my nametag. "Take another, Officer Goldsby, while I check to see. I'll be right back."

She took the two money orders and proceeded to what looked to be her manager's office, leaving me standing and doubting myself, wondering if there had been some type of trace placed on the remaining orders.

Dammit, what the fuck should I do? Should I wait this out, or should I just leave to gain what little of a head start I would have on the cops? To make matters worse, while the teller was in conversation with whom I'd taken to be the branch manager, the security guard got up to stand by the main door. Man, now that totally fucked me up! The small gesture of his made me even more suspicious and dampened what little strategy I had for an early exit. However, I figured out later he only changed positions because the lobby had begun to fill with its regular morning customers.

Finally, she returned, and believe me—I was nervous as hell. It wasn't tears dripping from my face this time, it was actually sweat. I used the back of my hand to dry my sweaty tears.

"I don't see a problem, sir," she said with a smile that seemed to be in my favor. "Although I'll need your ID. Just your military identification is appropriate. Then you can be on your way."

"Sure!" I said, much relieved, knowing that there wouldn't be a problem because that was the most used identification in my possession.

"Sir is there anything else we can help you with?" she asked after the transaction was complete, noticing what must have appeared to be a look of deep sadness on my face but was actually just nervousness and sweat. She seemed touched by my situation, and in the next moment she came from behind the counter with her arms wide open to give me a hug.

"Officer Goldsby, you be careful, and I'll keep you and your family in my prayers. If you need to, you could have a seat. I'll get you a cup of water."

Of course, I had lied about my uncle's death; however, by this phase of the game, Ms. Josie was caught up in the story, and I couldn't reverse what I had done. There was no turning back. So, to let you know, it wasn't all about making someone smile this time, but more along the lines of seeing how sympathetically deep a person's consciousness would become based on how they perceived my feelings.

The cop who I thought was not concerned about much had moved from the entrance to a stone column behind me. He then started to walk forward, and that confused me. Had he just been waiting for his moment? I didn't know whether or not those money orders had to be actually cashed before I could be apprehended. This was Washington, DC, and I was still under the impression that these people were better at capturing criminals than any other place in the world.

After she told me to have a seat, Ms. Josie just stood there with me, wondering if I was about to be caught and taken to jail. She had no concern about me being caught because she never realized I had done anything wrong. She had fallen for my story about my family's situation. Still, standing and facing her, my heart began to clatter like a set of pots and pans your grandmother moved around the bottom of her kitchen cabinet. As for the cop, he was still approaching, but it wasn't the cashing of the checks with which he was concerned.

He was caring and had become affectionate and warmhearted from what he was seeing and overhearing. He, too, was coming to shake my hand and offer his condolences.

"Come, Lieutenant Goldsby. I'll see you to the door." He then gave me a firm handshake, and I left.

These were postal-secured money orders, and by rule, with two forms of any valid photo identification (and I had seven sets of those), the money orders could be cashed at any state bank or federal post office. At that particular bank, however, I only needed one. I didn't make the law or set the damn rules. I just used them.

Chapter 14. New York's Arrival

Upon my return to New York, I had a strange and surprising encounter. It was early Tuesday morning on the first of February. While standing at the security window of the guard station to receive my parking permit and sticker, a guy walked past along the street who looked familiar. I wasn't sure, and I didn't want to look stupid by approaching him because I knew it couldn't be him, not Juncos in Queens. Plus, he just vanished out of sight.

A mirage maybe? Heck! We did spend an excessive amount of time together at work in Oklahoma, but a mirage? No. That carried no real relation to any state of reality.

I left the guard station and returned to the apartment. "Karol!" I hollered while walking into the bedroom.

"Yes," she said, emerging from the bathroom.

"Hey, Karol, I'm headed out to your brother's house. I realize you guys are off for the observation of Freedom Day, but would you care for anything on my way back?"

"No, I'm good. I'll finish studying, and later I'll go in for our eleven o'clock meeting."

"Okay, in that case, I'll grab DeVaan and take him with me. On the way back, I'll drop him off by your sister's since there is no school."

"Let her know I'll pick him up at three."

I had Newt from my previous job send me some information about Juncos. That was supposed to solidify the exact location of his scheduled distribution and logistics class. Orientation didn't start until ten o'clock, giving me plenty of time to get to Will's place and back. After arriving, he met me at his back porch and was holding the door open as we entered.

"Hey, Will, I come for that letter. I can't stay. You see, I have DeVaan with me."

"Yeah, I see. Here it is. Take it. I wouldn't want to see your time with him cut back any, so you better get your henpecked tail back in time."

After returning home, I got a chance to read the letter, which had to be a cover up letter for Juncos that read he had indeed been assigned to a distribution class for his company. Only to find out doing the course of the letter. The class had been scheduled for Sint Louis, Mo., not New York.

One thing was for sure ____I wasn't losing my damn mind after all. Knowing that, the next morning while walking to the bus stop several blocks away from our apartment complex, I wasn't surprised to find him.

"Juncos! What-ta you doing in Corona?" I yelled; this time sure it wasn't a mirage.

"I live in the Colombia apartments in Lefrak City. I'm on my way to the subway station. You coming?"

"Yeah!" I said with a little suspicion, and then asked. Why didn't you mention before that you lived here in Queens?" I asked while being a little confused, because neither of us had ever spoken about moving to New York, and it was almost impossible for both of us to be in the same school, and not only that but the same set of apartments. Juncos stood with his foot propped up on a street bench, smoking a joint. He wasn't particularly tall at around five-ten, but he had a huge chest and muscular arms, causing him to stand out. You couldn't tell he was Puerto Rican until he started to speak.

"Here, Vincent," he said as we waited for the bus. "You should hit this. It'll make your ride more relaxing."

He and I had never smoked a joint together, and I didn't care for any suspicion to be raised by my rejection. If he'd been advised on what he should say to me, then he already knew I smoked weed. I played along, but I wasn't buying into his game. It was too amazing for me. We both moved to the same city. Fine. It was the largest city in the country. But to be attending the same school and living not just in the same neighborhood but in the same damn apartment complex? Impossible. I believed in accidental situations, but ours was too much to accept to be a basic coincidence. There had to be an organized group behind it, pushing for it all to take place. I would have to pay close attention to Juncos going forward.

"Here, Juncos, try this fragrance. I use it all the time. It may cut down on the whiff people get from you when they pass."

Orientation wasn't long, but it was very interesting, and afterward, I made my way over to Barbizon to finish filling out more documents. It was during lunch, and I could see Ms. Lockhart, the instructor, leaving with a guy. He didn't notice me as I continued to the office to speak with Mrs. Tyler. Once I left her office, I headed to the subway station, and then home.

***

"Vincent." Karol's voice was much higher pitched than usual.

"In here, Karol. In DeVaan's room. What's wrong? Are you all right?"

"I'm fine, but do you know this guy?"

"Calm down, Karol. What guy?"

"This guy... who's on this card. He came by the bank yesterday and asked if I would give you this business card. He claims he once played professional football, but now he works for a company in Yonkers. He would like to sit with you later this evening to discuss a job offer. What about it?"

"First of all, Karol, I don't know him. He didn't give you any other information?"

"No, just this card."

"Well, here. I received this one the first day I registered for school. See if it matches the one you have."

85

I placed the card in her hand. "Yes! They're the same. How do these people know who you are? You've only been here for a minute." She was very curious but also impressed by what seemed to be taking place. "What do you think? Shouldn't we drive over to Yonkers to see if it's legit?"

"Think, Karol! How could it be legit? Think of what you just said."

"What? What did I say?"

Like everyone else who thought they knew me, Karol was no different. "Karol, you just said I've only been here for a minute, so how in the hell do these people know who I am?"

"True. How *do* they know?"

"I'm not sure. Their claim is the information they receive comes from a government affiliate with access to records of federal employees with outstanding work histories. I was briefly informed that I qualified for one of their work programs and was given that card, after which I never gave it another thought because these people knew me by name, and I had just arrived here the day before. Now, doesn't that sound a little farfetched?"

"Maybe a little, but wouldn't you like to find out? It could still have some legitimacy to it, wouldn't you think?"

"Hell naw! I'm here to go to school, not to join the damn mafia. But listen, if you really care to ride over there, it's fine with me. Let's go. We'll drop DeVaan off at his Aunt Mary's and find our way over there, but I'm telling you right now, I'm not accepting any type of job offer."

We proceeded to retrieve the Monte Carlo from the rooftop to make our way to Yonkers. While on our way, she asked, "Vincent, do you know Moke?"

"Yeah, what up with him?"

"He called earlier today while you were gone and told me to tell you that he'll be in Brooklyn this coming Sunday."

"A'ight."

"Man," she said, looking at this card, "it should be the next building on our right, but there's no parking out here. You should circle around the block. If there's nothing around there, maybe we should stop and ask someone. There could be a parking garage in the neighborhood."

I wondered about Karol's trust and honesty. She was clearly naïve. "Karol!" I said with a little hostility and resentment. "Are you sure about this? I'm not feeling like we should be over here."

"But Vincent, you just enrolled in two different schools. How're you intending to pay for them with no job?"

"I'm not sure, but job or no job, look at this place—it's guarded like a Rahway Prison camp. We should find our way out of here and back to Queens. Surely, Karol, it's understood the intelligence of yours is highly regarded, and you could be right that a job is needed. Though this is one time I feel that all of this should be up for farther discussion."

Karol was from the Deep South, across the railroad tracks over by the bayou, next door to the Praters, a very religious household where Reverend Prater would sing and minister to the entire community. "You're right, we should head back, but surely you'll have to get a job somewhere."

No one really knows how another individual thinks, but with the ties I had with her family and from the way she was raised, one could tell there wasn't a shred of dishonesty about her. Letting Karol continue the job hunt in Yonkers would be devastating to our relationship. She would find out things about me, way more than she needed to know, and I couldn't let that happen. The best option was to continue leading her toward the idea that eventually a job would surface and convince her that joining a so-called "government affiliate" could possibly be placing our family in danger. I decided the best I could do was to lead her into believing student loans were financing my tuition and whatever funds were left over could be used until a job became available. Even though the private investigation class and modeling school were paid in full, keeping that fact unknown was crucial. She knew I wasn't supposed to have that kind of cash. She hadn't long ago forwarded me a check for five hundred bucks, supposedly to help pay for my travel to New York. It never mattered how much money I had at any given time, I would always lead others to think I was broke. Flashy I wasn't, and I never gave a damn about being out front, or the first to pay, or making people think I was important.

The time had come to get away from Karol. I needed to place a call, and that couldn't be done with her in my company. Once we returned to the apartment after picking up DeVaan from his Aunt Mary's, I excused myself, concocting a story that the Monte Carlo was running a little warm and I needed to give it a look. The guard downstairs and I had become rather close, and his phone was always available to me for a marijuana joint tradeoff. And this was one particular time its use would come necessary 'cause I needed to reach out to Zo. Sitting on his money was risky.

A partner wasn't always in a position to front you six racks, so coming up with a plan to get him taken care of before something happened to his money was vital. *Maybe I could get several cashier's checks and mail them to him.* "Shit!" I said after giving that some thought. I'd just cashed multiple federal postal money orders, and moving twenty to twenty-five thousand dollars around in a bank within the same week with no job wouldn't be very smart, especially if it ever came time to defend myself as a result of the scheme.

I knew Valentine's Day weekend was coming soon, and I thought taking a chance to visit Natalie in Oklahoma wasn't a bad idea for the holiday. It would also give me a chance to check the status of Lola's graduation. Making good on Zo's package would be awesome, though achieving all of that could create a small problem if I weren't careful, knowing all along I didn't leave that area in good standing.

Getting jammed with Zach's little burglary caper, which resulted in the cops throwing down on Moke and me in a school zone, didn't end very nicely for all who were around me. After being bailed out by Lola and released from the county jail, she was put through several strenuous months of court appearances, lawyer meetings, and quite a few unannounced detective visits because of me.

They hounded her like she was part of the crime, trying to gather information that she really didn't have to offer. For all the harassment and court appearances, she decided to move out of our living arrangement and back on campus. Though I believe she may have fallen in love by then because she consented to traveling to Flint with me as soon as graduation was completed, not knowing at all into what she was headed. With the commitment to travel with me, it was imperative that I get in touch with her while on this visit.

Zo, on the other hand, was the main purpose of this Valentine's trip down south. I needed to get his money back to him. Heck! He was the only reason I was able to start school in New York in the first place. Not only that, but it would also give me that one chance to see Natalie again. I never let many people in on my feelings about Natalie. All I knew was, whenever this "It" that had control over my actions took hold, I wanted her within my grasp.

Chapter 15. A Plan to Return Zo's Package

I tap-tapped on the window, using my knuckles to awaken him. "Ali! Wake the heck up!" I hollered. With that, the window slid open. Ali was an individual who he and I had become close, he was one of the apartment's courtesy officers who loved most types of drugs. Though he was a hustler in his own way, and a serious one at that. Making a long-distance call cost a lot, and I couldn't do it from the apartment. He and I had made an agreement for the use of the security desk's office phone, I could pay with weed or whatever expensive drug available. The complex had a one eight hundred number in which you could have your party immediately return your call for free.

"You must need the phone."

"Yeah, I promise it won't take long."

"No problem. You know what it costs."

"Damn, Ali. Here, take this."

"What is this? It's rolled like a darn piece of paper."

"Don't worry, it's a little triple threat. The weed is stuffed with dual chemicals, though, so you better be careful 'cause you always talking about people's shit don't be good. Oh, and take these—it's a half sheet of five squares of the plastic acid. Be careful they are stronger than they look."

"Dang! I thought you said it wouldn't take long?"

I passed it all over to him as I picked up the phone and carried it into the small utility room. "It won't. Just be careful with that stuff."

I dialed. "Natalie, please."

"This is she. May I help you?"

"Hey, Nae!" I replied, using the nickname I'd started calling her.

"Is this Vincent?"

"Yeah, how are you?"

"I'm good. I wasn't expecting a call until March."

"True, but listen—I'm planning a trip there for Valentine's weekend, and I would love nothing more than to spend some time with you. I won't be able to stay for Valentine's Day, but will you be around that Saturday?"

"No, Vincent. I've made plans to spend Valentine's week with my mother in Baton Rouge, but are you sure you'll be able to come?"

"Yes, I'm positive."

"Okay, in that case, the visit with my mom can be canceled because that week is her shop's busiest time of year for doing hair, and she'd be cutting her appointments short just to spend time with me. If your itinerary is complete for arrival, let me know, and I'll pick you up from the airport."

I couldn't let her do that. The entire trip was based on getting in touch with Zo in order to lock down his payment. I didn't want to be around Natalie anytime I wasn't being strictly legal, and getting off the plane with over twenty grand of Zo's money was a bit risky.

"I've already arranged to be picked up. I'll be in Friday afternoon with a meeting scheduled that evening. Once the meeting is over, I'll give you a call."

I didn't have a meeting scheduled, nor did I have any flight reservations. But if I couldn't see her on this trip, I probably wouldn't make the trip at all. I'd figure out another way to get Zo his money. There was something special about Natalie, and I would do anything within my power to see her. I knew it wasn't time for her to be a part of my life given the way I was living, but I was willing to keep her close and wait until that time came to fruition. This was my one chance to see Natalie again, and possibly my last. Being away from her for so long, I was taking a chance of losing her for good. But returning to New York to complete the private investigator school was the only thing on my mind. To me, it was a must, and I wasn't turning back.

"Sounds good, Vincent, but don't let me down."

"I gotcha."

Once the visit with her was confirmed, I focused on reaching out to Lola. Lola was someone I definitely needed to contact. With her graduation coming soon, spending some valuable time with her before leaving that weekend was important. If I were to be successful at the hustle game, Lola would be the one I needed. She had me convinced that she would roll with me, and my destination didn't matter to her.

Karol, on the other hand, had just recently graduated from Grambling State University and begun a fast-paced career of her own in New York. She had set the bar high and her standards even higher. Her goals were so high, they almost seemed unreachable. She had a determination and desire that was remarkable, and for me to disrupt any of her plans would have been selfish.

I liked my fast-paced life, and I loved the feeling quick schemes gave me. Honestly, the money never meant much to me. I would spend it just as fast as I made it. The thrill of doing wrong was what steered me, and once my ideas became a reality, I'd find myself relaxed. To be honest, I think Karol knew right away, as did I, that we were headed in two different directions. I was sure she could see something was not right with me, and more than likely, we wouldn't be able to survive a long-term stay with one another. She should be praised, though, for letting me live with them and giving me the opportunity to attend school. She happened to be one of the smartest people I knew, and that was a huge circle.

I was almost sure that she was carrying the same affection for me as she once did. And for me to involve her in a life of crime would have been terribly wrong, especially since she had such high expectations and ambitious goals for herself. She was just as aggressive and much smarter than me, but no matter how hard she tried to pull me up to her standards, that "It," whatever it was, would sever my ability to hold on while she pulled. I had no power over what was guiding me wrong, but I did know if I could cut back on the consumption of these powerful and evil drugs, just maybe I could start figuring this "It" out.

The next two weeks would be the most difficult for me—I planned to attend two schools, and I had no intention of letting anything get in the way of that.

When done in New York, my goal was to return to Flint, Michigan. I had some unfinished business over there. One time in Flint, I was stopped for a traffic violation in my Cobra Mustang, then taken to a police precinct downtown where I was accused of a bank robbery. Not only did they hold me for nearly thirty-six hours, shuffling me back and forth from a holding cell to their interrogation room, but it was also done without producing any type of substantial evidence for their claim. I was eventually released, promised a ride home for the misunderstanding, placed in a squad car, and taken to Pierson Road, where I was told to get out. I was in total shock, standing there in three to four inches of snow, shivering with enough anger to kill. That was when I decided to accept it was time for me to leave Flint.

In addition to all that, I couldn't gather where in the hell the information they did have on me had come from. It was obvious someone knew something, and I didn't see the value of continuing my stay after the harassment. Actually, it was like a violation of human and personal rights, jamming someone up in a damn interrogation room and holding them there for nearly thirty-six hours with no food, no shower, not even enough water to drink—all because of some information that carried no valid proof I had anything to do with what they were claiming. Only two people had knowledge of the banking incident in question, and one of them was already dead. And under no circumstances was I revealing a word about anything, even if something had been mentioned to someone before the death of that individual. He was now gone, meaning it was null and void, leaving them with only hearsay and not enough information to continue any type of investigation. Indeed, it had come time to leave, but I secretly knew in my mind one day I would return and maybe deliver to them what they had accused me of.

As for Lola, as stated earlier, it was important I reach out to her on my visit. She was the type all the hustlers and so-called gangsters were looking to grasp. There was a special mystique about her that was interesting and kept others wondering. She loved to strut with her blouse tied in a bowtie-style knot that showed off her deeply sunken belly button. Her 5'8" frame was bottomed beautifully with long, slender legs, highlighting a walk that everybody admired. Her skin was alluring, her teeth were sparkling white, and her otherworldly smile left people stunned, wondering what she was all about. But most of all, she had a tenacious way of getting next to whoever or whatever she wanted.

She was a very sought-after gem, and from what I was hearing, one of the most notorious gangsters on the streets wanted her, but she also carried an attitude that was exceptionally hard to deal with. With all that said, Lola had her strong points, too—she was very smart, with a great business mind, and most of all, she was with me. I couldn't do anything but cherish how she had my back, and for that, I would protect her, no matter where we went. Once this mission in New York was over, I'd be headed back to Flint. My intentions once we arrived there may not be those of a normal person, though being convinced by Lola that she was game to travel with me was fueling my already dangerous and mischievous thoughts. She was the right fit for my outlandish plan. Heck! Sometimes the things I'd catch myself doing would surprise me. Was it really the drug that had me, or was it the "It" that was controlling every damn thing I did? Because I wasn't only addicted to the drugs. Along with that, I had a serious criminal illness, a disease that was completely out of control. I knew it, but there wasn't anything I could do to stop it.

The call ended, and before returning the phone to him, I said, "Ali, those acid squares, are potent. I would sell them all if I were you, a half of one is more than enough for one individual to consume."

Chapter 16. A Special Visit

There were only a few days left before Valentine's Day weekend. We had been in school for almost two weeks now, and leaving for a business trip wasn't a problem. Karol seemed to be really happy with my being there with them as a family and everything going as well as it had.

Still, I needed to proceed with the plan to get Zo his money back, and adding to the visit Logan just to see if I could increase the split that I would receive from Zo, wouldn't hurt. Not only that, but my arrival would also give me a chance to visit others who I really needed to see that weekend. After the reservation was finally made and all other plans were taken care of, I flew out to Oklahoma. Once the plane landed at the airport, I waited for Zo.

It was late evening on Friday, February 11, and I was passing some time at the corner of the bar, having a mild drink and watching the entrance of the cocktail lounge. Zo was late, but my Southern Comfort on the rocks was keeping me calm, even though I was beginning to get a little angry. I had given him the exact time and place where we would meet.

I decided to find a phone and call Logan. I needed to know what a good time would be to meet with him on campus. Afterward, I returned to the lounge, and finally, having sat for much longer than I wanted, I stood and turned toward the exit door to leave. There was Zo, standing with those bowed legs, laughing, and joking with Sonny. I wasn't expecting Sonny to be with him, but it was always nice to see another homie. Both Sonny and Zo were from Monroe, Louisiana, and sometimes when traveling home to Ferriday, I would stop by Monroe just to chat with them.

"Smooth! My dude!" said Sonny, the first to enter the lounge.

"Sonny! Hey, Zo!"

"What up, Smooth?"

"Man, you late again."

"Heck, I'll tell you what—I'll swap these slow and bowlegs with you, then maybe I'll be on time."

"Man! You're funny. What's cooking, you guys?" I asked.

"Heck, Smooth," Sonny answered. "Not much. Bout the same as you left it, but how's the Big Apple?"

"Dang, Sonny. It's remarkable. Would you believe I'm paying thirty dollars a month to ride the subway to school every day? Hey! And another thirty dollars a month just to park the Monte Carlo on the rooftop of a damn building."

"Well, you got-ta do some serious hustling 'cause New York sounds expensive. Hey, Smooth, speaking of hustling—would you be interested in twenty fully automatic machine guns?"

After taking a serious look around, I said, "Dang! Not here, Sonny. Would you guys' care for a late lunch?"

"Yeah," they answered in unison.

"Oh! By the way, Zo—your package is in this briefcase sitting next to me. Take it with you when we leave. Another thing—in the morning after we share a nice breakfast, will you take me to the Skirvin Hotel? I'm meeting Natalie there."

"The Skirvin Hotel!" Zo shouted. "Why the Skirvin?"

"Heck, Zo, after what you put me through with that money order scheme... showing Natalie a fun time and spending the night at a luxurious hotel for Valentine's weekend is the least I can do for her."

"Damn! Smooth, that's where all the financial bankers and gangster politicians hang out. Shit, she must be special." Even Zo could tell my feelings toward Natalie were much different than they were for the others we had been around.

***

Natalie and I spent a wonderful Saturday afternoon together, bouncing around Oklahoma City as joyful and happy as a couple could be. I think both of us knew there was something special about us. While finishing her shopping at the shoe store—she loved to shop for shoes—I could tell she would love nothing more than a chance to spend more time with me, especially as a couple living together. But no, the strength of her female intuition wouldn't allow for that because she had come to the conclusion that there was something seriously wrong with me. Even though she knew this about me, the love she had was too strong to ignore. Still, there was something even stronger than her intuition—an uncontrollable force that kept me attracted to her. With her realizing all of this, the only thing she could do for us was to love me from afar, and that she did.

Returning to our room, Natalie was in the mood. She got freshened up and returned from the bathroom wearing nothing but her birthday suit and a fitted Skirvin bathrobe. She was a very discrete person and had been that way for as long as I had been around her. Only once previously had she shared herself with me, and even then, she would only undress in the dark.

She exited the bathroom, moving somewhat slower than usual, and for the first time, I was completely lost for words. She was sexy and stacked. God had gifted her with everything others were wishing for, and she'd been hiding it. She continued to walk toward me as I lay flat on my back in bed, confused and amazed at her actions while she slowly crawled in, knees straddling my body, her hairy labia right on top of me... so unlike the lady I knew.

"Vincent, you know we're not together much. Please be understanding."

"Sure, Nae. You're very special to me." I sat up, placing my chest next to her breast. "I'll be gentle."

Once our chests were separated, I lay flat on my back and decided to make this right with her. She was different, and I wanted to prove to her___ not only did she know, but so did I. Romantically,

I would give her every inch of my body in a loving affair and to be honest I wanted too. But no, I decided to lay gentle while discussing how valuable our relationship could be in the future, with her making what passionate moves there were. Afterward, we lay there sharing a lovely and sweet conversation until she mentioned it was getting close to dinnertime. "Vincent, I think we should refresh ourselves, even if we're only removing the sweat from our bodies. We have a reservation." Even then, she was still the punctual type.

"Heck, Natalie, I'm already full," I joked.

"Well, you better hope they have a slider burger for you downstairs because I'm hungry after all the work I just put in."

I giggled, and we both started laughing.

She removed herself from the bed and headed to the bathroom. I watched as she surprisingly strutted freely across the room.

Once we were cleaned and dressed, we stepped out into the hall, still chuckling on our way to the elevator.

"A slider burger, huh?"

"You better hope."

Finally, we stepped inside the dining room and were immediately seated. The dinner was magnificent—wonderful food and some of the finest wine offerings in America. The great meal in Skirvin's unique dining room, enjoyed while being entertained by live music, had me feeling some kind of way. We turned in early that evening expecting a night of good rest in preparation for an early-morning church service.

But it turned out our unforgettable evening together at the Skirvin Hotel wasn't over. Throughout the night, we would awake and begin fooling around. I was fatigued the following morning, but who cared about being exhausted after a night like that? As for Natalie, she seemed refreshed after taking an early shower.

"How're you feeling this morning, Natalie?"

"I'm good! We must visit the Skirvin again someday. It's a beautiful place."

"You're not tired?"

"Why, Vincent? Why would I be tired?"

"Natalie, we were up most of the night."

"Sure, we were, though I thought you enjoyed it. I know I did."

"You bet I did, and you surprised me the whole night."

"Great, then you can surprise me by attending church service with me. Can you do that?"

"Consider it done," I said, smiling.

"Come, we have plenty of time, and if the service is as good as the past evening we shared together, then we're in for a treat."

I wondered for many years about that night, finding out a couple of decades later that the Skirvin Hotel was thought to be haunted and tended to leave visitors wondering about weird sounds and unknown voices they claimed to have heard while staying at the lavish hotel.

I must say, none of that happened with us, but whatever may have pushed Natalie into her erotic desire to touch me throughout the night, it came with the utmost pleasure of enjoyment. I loved it every time she rolled over.

Now she seemed so happy, glowing as we left the hotel and made our way to her Mustang coupe. Once we arrived at the church, I parked and politely went around to open her door. I was making sure the feeling she had would continue.

The service was early, but I enjoyed it almost as much as I enjoyed the look on her face as she smiled so abundantly. Afterward, it was time for her to drop me off at Newt's place before taking off for Baton Rouge, where she was headed to visit her mother on Valentine's Day. At Newt's place, I gave Natalie a little kiss on her cheek and exited the car.

"I'll call when I think you've arrived at your mother's. Are you all right with that?"

"Sure, I'll be expecting your call." With that, she pulled away, and I stood and watched until finally, she was out of sight.

Once inside, I asked Newt about Lola.

"So, you don't know?"

"All I know is when I try talking to her, she seems distant. I haven't been able to get much out of her. Is there something I'm missing?"

"She hasn't been doing good. Beverly, her roommate, has been taking her back and forth to the doctor."

"Did she say why she's been taking her to the doctor?"

"No. She doesn't go into details with me."

"Do you have Beverly's number?"

"Yeah, no problem. We just finished talking before you arrived."

"Will you call? I need to see if I can get something out of her."

"Yeah, I'll see if she's still there." He picked up the phone and dialed. "Beverly, it's Newt. Vincent is here. He needs to speak with you. Here, Smooth."

I was relieved she was still home and had picked up because there was no other method of contacting her if she wasn't there. Now my nervous system was in overdrive. *Shit. I should have kept trying to reach out to Lola while I was there in New York.*

"Hey, Beverly, I'm sorry for bothering you, but what's going on with Lola? Newt told me you've been taking her to see a doctor. Is she all right?"

"Darn, Vincent, if you had been here and not been running all around the damn country, you would know. It's a damn shame you've been gone since Christmas. She hasn't seen and barely heard from you."

"Hell, Beverly, I get that, but what's wrong with her?"

"She's pregnant!"

"What?"

"Yes, and her body is not accepting it well. She's been ill. She's struggling, Vincent, trying to carry this child alone so you can be successful and not have to worry while attending school. Man, all she talks about is having your child, finishing her semester, and being prepared to leave when you return. But she's afraid, Vincent."

"Why?"

"Because you vowed to keep in touch, but you haven't. Making things even more difficult, she thinks you're leaving for Flint without them. Man, you need to call her. She's worried to death."

"Damn! You're on point, Beverly. I'll get it done right away."

"You should! She's at her parents' house in Arkansas."

I spent several hours making numerous calls, trying to get in touch with Lola. Finally, I got through to her. Things were different than what I had pictured—she was lively and full of energy. Like the Lola I knew, not the sick, solemn person Newt and Beverly had described.

"Vincent!"

Since she didn't sound weak or even sick at all, I played along. "It's been a minute. How's it going? Where're you now?"

"I'm here in Edmond. I came to visit for the weekend."

"I had no idea you'd be out of town."

"How could you? You hardly ever call, and you act as though we don't exist."

"What-ta you mean, 'we don't exist'?"

"I'm pregnant, Vincent!"

"Pregnant! You mean, like, with our child?"

I couldn't let her know Beverly had already informed me. That wouldn't have been right. Plus, I could tell that she was trying to mislead me about her true health.

"Apparently so, and I've been wanting to tell you, but every time you called you were in a rush, and I didn't want to bother you. It's been very difficult on me without you being around. Man! You just went and left, leaving me there alone, and that hurt. Now the doctors are telling me that it's very possible I may not be able to carry to full term, but I'm fighting, and I will continue to fight. With you being forced to leave town in such a rush and me pregnant at the same time, I felt it would be too much on you. Though you still could have called more, and maybe I wouldn't be as stressed. Two months since you fled, Vincent."

"True, and I apologize for that."

"And I'm sorry that I kept this from you."

Her point of view was shifting as she opened up to me. She began acting like she had done something wrong. Maybe it was unfair to carry a child and not let the father know, but it was my fault I got caught up and left her like I did. Once I realized and clearly understood what she was going through, it moved me into more of a committed urgency to keep in touch with her. And after our conversation, it became clear to me that she had a strong determination and desire to deliver our child.

I must say, after coming off the high of being with Natalie, falling to such an extreme and devastating low was brutal, even for a guy like me, especially after finding out Lola was having such a difficult time. People would often say to me, "Man, it's like you don't have a heart," but hell, even I had feelings, and this was one time I could envision what hurt actually felt like. She was hurting inside, and with the probability of losing a child, she couldn't possibly hide that hurt. My job was to make sure she kept faith and stayed strong while going through such challenging times. Lola had physical complications, though I think just hearing from me strengthened her mentally and gave her the sense of security that I would soon return for them.

"That's okay, Lola. I understand and promise to keep in touch from now on."

"Vincent, you've always been a person who stands behind what he says. I'll be looking for you when the semester is over."

"Don't worry, Lola. I'll be here."

"Sounds good and take care of yourself."

Chapter 17. A Special Visit, Part Two

With Lola absent from town, I had extra time to spend with Newt and other friends. One in particular was Logan, with whom I had carried out wrongful activities with, for years. The rest of my time would be shared with Regina. She, too, was having a difficult time after the passing of her mom. She and I had become more than just friends. We were like siblings who had experienced so much together. My love for her was beyond normal, and what I had done involving her in all of those crime schemes was demoralizing and wrong. If only I had known our acquaintance would have become such a treasure, using an enemy would have been better suited to my purposes. Realizing the danger, I put her in, making sure she was okay was important to me. Mind you, she got caught up early in her banking career, and quick money, a lot of it, would alter the minds of most individuals. I could tell she was still worried about getting caught. And, assuring her once again she had nothing to worry about was critical.

She had been extremely careful and was good at doing her job. Over the duration of our work together, other than the inside bank jobs that she had control over, there was no other reason for her to worry. For all those outside drive-through transactions, Zo and I had kept her completely clear. Not once did we ever have her cash a single drive-through check or money order or make any type of bank draft—anything that would tie the three of us together.

Our relationship was a cherished one, and it had been more than three years since our meeting at the hotel barroom when I'd promised never to place her in harm's way. I'd honored that promise, and needless to say, a goodbye was appropriate, and I wanted to let her know the love I had for her would stand for a lifetime. But in order for us to stay safe, our ties to one another had to end.

It was a gorgeous, spring-like day for the time of year. With Natalie gone and Lola out of town, Newt and I were alone, with him preparing a Cajun-style gumbo for dinner. He was a good friend from New Orleans and was still the messenger and mail clerk for the company I formerly worked for. Now I was trying to explain my strange situation with Juncos to him.

"Are you telling me that Juncos is in New York?"

"Yeah."

"Damn! I knew he was supposed to be gone for a few months to attend some type of logistics and distribution class for the company. Only his class was scheduled for St. Louis, not New York, ya-heard."

"Yeah, I got that from the letter you sent. But he's in New York. Why?"

"That could be for any reason, Smooth. A conference, a company meeting, but what I do know is he'll be returning to take over our logistics department when his class is over. So, what you're telling me doesn't seem strange at all."

"Maybe not, Newt, but this dude is attending the same school and is living on the same block and in the same apartment complex as I am. Dammit, man, you don't think something's peculiar about that?"

"Not really. All of that seems possible, ya-heard, but what's strange to me is that I'm positive his class was scheduled to take place in St. Louis."

"Okay, Newt. If that's not enough to convince you, what about us both taking the same private investigator's course? Would that be considered a little suspicious?"

"Look, dude, either you're overly drugged and hallucinating, or you're under serious surveillance. My suggestion for you would be to stay clear of Juncos if you think something is up with him. He's a guy who worked under your tutelage and is very close to you. Could he have lifted your detailed information somehow?"

"It's possible, though I have no proof. But there is one thing for sure—none of that stuff that's happening with him is coincidental."

"Yo, Smooth, we've been together for how long now?"

"Several years... why?"

"'Cause we've escaped a lot and take it from me—I think God was trying to tell us something in that accident. Man, we should have never gotten out of your Road Runner alive. Why don't you give it a break? You could finish your investigative class since that's what you like. Grab your diploma and start your own business. You don't seem to be doing well working for others, and you can't continue doing wrong. Eventually, you *will* be stopped, ya-heard!

"And not only that, but all the drugs you consume... I believe they're taking a toll on your body. Man, sometimes I worry. You don't think you've become addicted to that TAC? Look at yourself, you're all skin and bone, and your temple has a very short fuse. You don't think something is wrong with you?"

"No! I'm fine. I can handle it."

"Smooth, you are not fine! What about the women? Do you ever pay attention to what you do to them? Dude, it's like you're spinning them around through a revolving door in the middle of a metropolitan building, waiting for whoever's turn it is___ to exit. Slowly, Smooth, you are becoming a serial womanizer. Especially with the way you're in and out of women's lives, you treat them as though they have no quality or value. Smooth! You're not only addicted to drugs, but you're also addicted to women... man, you should *stop* it. Maybe you should get some counseling of some kind."

"Damn, Newt! Counseling? I thought you were my friend. Now you're calling me crazy?"

"No! I'm not calling you crazy, but as a friend, I think you should at least consider that the drugs may be taking over your frame of thought."

My spiritual side could hear everything Newt was trying to tell me. I just couldn't stop the "It" that was inside me. My persona, a curse... whatever the f**k this "It" was seemed stronger than anything my mother had taught me. I had no control.

"That gumbo smells good, Newt," I said, deciding to change the subject.

"What-ta bout a sample before you get out-ta here?"

"Cool! Any large crab boiling in that pot?"

"Yeah, mon! Nawlins-style from the Gulf shores, ya-heard!"

"All right, Newt. Just a small bowl. Hey, is it okay to use your phone? I need to holler at Regina. Hopefully, she'll be able to take me to the college. Logan promised he'd wait for me."

"See? There you go again! You never seem to quit. You and Logan will soon end up in trouble if you guys don't stop."

"Dang, Newt. You worry too much. We'll be fine."

I gathered from our last conversation that Logan had been awarded his own chemistry lab. This dude was successful. He had gotten his doctorate and became a professor at the university. The first chemistry lab he used was extraordinary enough. I could only imagine what a new and modern lab would look like. Regina and I had visited Logan sometimes in the past when he was still in grad school. She would always help in financing some of the higher end transactions for us.

"Regina speaking. May I help you?"

"Yes, this is—"

"Vincentius!" she yelled. "Mr. Smooth himself. You never have to tell me who you are. There's only one. How are you?"

"I'm decent. I'm here in town. Are you busy?"

"Vincent, even if I were, no way I wouldn't find time for you. Where the heck are you?"

"Over by Newt's place."

"You stay there. I'll be right over."

I was surprised when Regina showed up in a new burgundy 1977 Chevy Vega GT.

"What do you think, Vincent?"

"I love it, but damn, Regina. It's a five-speed."

"That's right, and don't just stand there—come on, hop in. I had to get a stick. After you demolished the gorgeous Road Runner, it was a no-brainer. Now, where to, and how long are you here for?"

"I have a plane to catch later this evening, but right now, could you run me by Logan's? I won't be there long, and then we can stop by our favorite spot. I have a Valentine's gift for you."

"A gift is fine, but man, do you ever think about giving up the hustling? It's scary, Vincent. Every day there's a feeling like a body of officers is coming to arrest me. Are we really clear of all those transactions?"

"Yes, Regina! You're going to be fine. It's been over five months since our last transaction. You would have heard something by now. But whatever you do, don't get conned into any scheme with Zo. It's too dangerous. Without a doubt, you'll get in trouble."

"Don't worry about me," she said. "My criminal stint is over, and I'm still trying to understand how I let you talk me into it. Vincent, you may not look, talk, or even act like anybody who's trying to be cool, but there's something about you that enthralls others, especially if given the opportunity to hang around you long enough. By the way, you can believe me—that FBI agent didn't lie when he placed that 'Smooth' title on you."

"Maybe I'm not all of those things but being in your company makes me feel good about all my shortcomings. Because with those beautiful blue eyes and your magnificent personality, you are as pretty as they come." She was, and her amazing character camouflaged all the wrong she had done.

"Thanks. I appreciate the compliment."

"Sure. Now come! This won't take long. Logan's waiting on me. I called him already from the airport."

We left in her little Vega and zoomed over to his all-new chemistry lab. Once we were finally inside, Logan greeted us immediately.

"Regina! I must say—it's been a while. How are you?"

"I'm fine, Professor Flannigan. Doesn't that sound good, being called professor? I see you're still manufacturing your products, though."

"Yes, it does, and yes, I am. Are you still in the finance business?" he joked.

"No! My criminal services are no longer available," she shot back, and we all giggled.

"Smooth, it's nice to know you're doing good as well. Everything is in this one container, and it's been medically packed and wrapped specifically for you. The price is set, but I'm throwing in extra as a gift. Frankly, I've never forgotten that first ride you gave me to pick up my car after school that evening. Smooth, do you realize we've been friends well over three years now, and not once have we ever had an argument or confrontation of any kind? Though I'm saying that to say this—those pills, please be aware they are near deadly. I've branded and shaped them as Dilaudids, but they're much stronger than a regular Dilaudid. I've injected those with a powerful drug Smooth, called carfentil that has not yet been legally approved to be introduced into the veterinary world of medicine. Now for the drug of choice that you truly love so much the powder TAC, it too, is deadly if not taken properly. Though, I've reduced the dosage on it, as several complaints have surfaced, of holes burning through the tissue of user's nostrils. However, it is still a drug to pay close attention to too. And now for you, figuring out the best travel solution for the package may be just as dangerous as the drugs are deadly. Because, it's a lot to travel with, you must be careful how you manage your return trip home without getting caught."

"Okay, thanks, and I appreciate the wrap."

We sat for a few minutes to catch up, and afterward, Regina and I departed with a package containing three thousand pills with special ingredients added, and shaped in the form of Dilaudids, plus three ounces of TAC fabricated specifically for me.

Combine those two drugs___ later, with two pounds of RedBud that Newt was throwing in for free, would secure my financial situation for a while. Getting it all back to New York seemed a bit chancy, though. Fitting it all in my newly purchased gym bag wasn't a problem but transporting it back to the city without getting caught could prove a challenge. My mind wandered a bit until a solution surfaced—I'd purchase some luggage for instance, a large footlocker and have it all shipped.

After picking up the marijuana from Newt, I rolled it, and the specially wrapped package of drugs from Logan, inside a large blanket. I would then place it all inside a beautiful gold trim oversized "hope chest" and purchase a ticket. A bus ticket... I decided to let it all travel alone to New York by bus, making sure it was oversized with dimensions beyond the acceptance of UPS. The bus terminal wasn't as strict either and the cost wasn't nearly as much to ship as it would be by freight truck. Plus, the beauty of the "hope chest remove most if not all suspicion of what it might hold. Once my bus ticket was purchased the oversized chest would be loaded in the bottom storage area of the bus with a claim number. You'd retrieve it at its destination from the baggage claim area of the bus terminal with the same ticket number, when it finally arrives. Any transporting of drugs was risky and dangers, you'd have to pick your poison in how you got it done. Than hope for the best that your one time shipment would make the trip, without interference.

"Dang, Vincent! You never cease to amaze me with the things you do. Are you ever frightened?"

"Yes, but who wants to be around someone who doesn't fear anything, Regina. A person who doesn't fear is a person destined to ashes. They're either living among those who are institutionalized and surrounded by what's built from ash, or they have returned to ashes themselves. The lack of fear is very dangerous.

"To me, fear is the recognition of a God, a reverence, a feeling of deep respect for something supernatural. If you don't fear what you do, you won't last long doing it. Just as you feared and decided to quit, I fear, but without the power to achieve control, I can't do the same. I can't quit. But I know what's done wrong can't be done long, so I move on."

"Speaking of moving on, why don't we pass on our favorite spot? I've already prepared dinner, so why don't we stop by the house? You can relax, eat something, and show me this gift you're supposed to have for me. You're hungry, right?"

"Sure, 'cause that one Cajun crab in that bowl, at Newt's has vanished."

"Sounds good, and after everything's over, I'll take you back to Newt's place. And... I do understand that this will probably be our last visit together."

Regina was right, and she had begun to cry, accepting that this would be our final meeting. She was like a dear sister to me, and I continuously thought of her throughout my life. Once the meal was over and we spent some more time catching up, I gave her a beautiful pink winter beanie with the word "SMOOTH" embroidered in black. The cap represented her two favorite people—her mom, who had passed away from cancer, and a special brother, me, who would forever remember her.

"Wow! Vincent, two hours have gone by. We have to get over by Newt's to get your things and head out to the airport."

"Dang, Regina, I didn't realize the time," I said, looking up at the clock on the wall, which hung above two decent-sized pictures—one of Jesus and the other of her mother—that sat on the fireplace mantle.

Once there, she followed Newt and me to the airport, refusing to accept the visit at her house to be the last one. She walked with me to get checked in and then waited with us until the flight number was called to depart.

"Get up!" she said. "It's hard to hug someone setting down."

It was our last hug. I never saw Regina again.

Chapter 18. New York

I was the first to enter the plane, and while walking toward my seat, it became obvious to me that a plan to disperse a portion of the drugs must take place upon my arrival. Logan had sold these Dilaudids to me, a thousand of them to be exact, at five bucks each. They were much better than the acid pills everyone was using. This was the new drug of choice, and they were selling these on the streets up north for anywhere between fifty to one hundred dollars each, easily creating a sizable profit for anyone who would distribute them. My other goal was to take most of the weed Newt had given to me free and roll it into individual joints laced with TAC.

Upon returning to New York after brainstorming during a successful flight, I planned to set up a meeting with Agent, my friend in South Jersey. Agent and I had been good friends for years, and he was always willing to collect on a quick and easy hustle. Selling him five hundred pills for ten bucks each and two ounces of TAC for three grand apiece would be like a gift to him. Everyone hearing about the drug wanted it, but getting it was something more difficult. This Dilaudid was probably the most potent pill around, claimed Logan. He explained to me up front that the pill was already more powerful than morphine, and the added spice of carfentil made them near deadly. The chance of getting his hands on five hundred of them would be hard for Agent to turn down, and realizing all of that, I called him. It was late Sunday night, but who cared?

"My dude," he said, seemingly with a little more tenor to his voice after realizing it was me.

"Mr. Car Manager himself. What up wit-cha?" I asked.

"Trying to make an honest living, my dawg. What-ta you up to?"

"Not much, just checking to see if you're interested in a small lick?"

"Usually, Vincent, coming from you, I would say yes. But what's my cost, and how much on the cap?"

"Eleven grand for the package. Five hundred Dilaudids and two ounces of TAC, uncut."

"Huh! You serious, dude?"

"Yeah! You ever known me not to be?"

"No! Not really, but when can I get it?"

"What about this coming Saturday? Will you be ready?"

"Sure, where?"

"Princeton! Could you meet me at the Square in Princeton, New Jersey, at six in the morning?"

"No problem. I gotcha."

Shit! All I could do was hope everything would go well because what was left of the fifteen grand of the thirty thousand split with Zo was nearly gone. Thanks to the six grand I owed him for school, five thousand for the pills, and three thousand for the TAC, suddenly I was all but broke.

Recouping eleven grand from Agent for the drugs would keep me from any strenuous type of hustling. It would also give him a chance to flip the total package and easily double his lick on just the pills alone if that's what he chose to do. That would be the easiest thing for him to accomplish, but between the pills and the uncut TAC estimated street value soaring to around sixty to near seventy-five thousand dollars... would leave anyone struggling with whether or not they should flip the drugs or deal them in the streets.

Heck, it was close to 11:00 p.m. when I finally pulled into my personal parking spot. I exited the Monte Carlo and made my way down and back up to the apartment, finding Karol still sitting up at the kitchen table studying. I quickly said hello and headed straight to the bedroom, knowing it would be the first place she'd go once she finished her work, and I set the gift I'd bought on her pillow. I'd been gone for several days, and to return with nothing would have been disrespectful.

The next day was Valentine's Day and I had been gone since Friday. So, I hurried to the bathroom to take a quick shower. When done, I slipped into a pair of PJs and headed to DeVaan's room. I could see that Karol had left the kitchen table, and I called for DeVaan to follow me. Together, we peeked in on Karol, who was reading the card. We giggled as we watched her pick up the box and then headed back to DeVaan's room. Afterward, she appeared in the doorway, looking surprised but happy for sure.

"Vincent, the box of Millionaires was a lovely gift, and the card is gorgeous. Thank you! You made my day."

DeVaan and I looked at her while sitting on his bed together. Then I said to him, "Why don't we give her a hug?"

We rushed over and seized her in a gigantic, tight, wraparound squeeze.

"You two are bringing the best out of me, but DeVaan—it's time for you to hit the sack."

The morning arrived. It was Valentine's Day, Monday the fourteenth, and Karol was up ready and was headed off to work with a feeling of joy. DeVaan had already been placed on the bus for school, as I had slept in because of the long weekend of travel I'd done. Still, I had to make my way to school.

Chapter 19. Hustling at School

Unbeknownst to my fellow classmates, my friend Moke had been in the city for a couple of weeks now. He would meet me in an alley behind the school at lunch break, we would quickly swap the toothpick sized joints that he would bring with him for the money I'd received from the students. Afterward he'd proceed ahead of me, to the park carrying with him my portable three-card monte table and the money for the pre-rolled joints.

Then I would return and wait for the others to finish taken care of business and using the restroom, as we all would walk to the park together. This is when the preordered joints receive from Moke would be passed out along the way, to all those who had ordered. Even Juncos would preorder, but it always seemed to bother him more than the others that it was never a direct transaction of money for the weed with him.

During lunch break, I would shuffle the cards on my table to gain attention. Moke would then walk up to the table as a regular from the crowd and win, convincing others they could find the correct card and do the same. The three-card monte con game, as I called it, was fun and very intriguing, and most of my classmates would meet in Washington Square Park every day to either try their luck at winning or watch me shuffle the cards briskly. It looked simple, but the designated card never seemed to end up where you would think. But to have success, it was prudent to randomly choose an individual from the crowd and let them win. This part of the game was very important in controlling the interest of everyone who had gathered.

The card scheme itself could make eighty to a hundred bucks on any given day. Combining that with the marijuana hustle, which brought in another seventy to eighty dollars daily, had both of us hooked. It was a problem, though, getting the marijuana distributed because there wasn't an easy way without direct sales, which was something I refused to commit to. What we were doing was much slower on the profit end, but it kept Moke and me really busy and out of trouble. Lacing TAC in those toothpick-sized joints had everybody in the park who tried them buzzing with excitement.

I was approached by others who had tested the weed and wanted to purchase straight from me, but product-to-them, cash-to-me was something I was truly against. I had never sold to anyone through direct sales. But figuring, since the toothpick joints being passed out only to my classmates were doing so well, a strategy to enhance that was needed and what a strategy it was.

Moke showing up every day made things function a lot smoother, and I accepted his hunger, his need for cash. He couldn't find work in Brooklyn, and from my understanding, one who doesn't work will eventually do wrong. Moke wasn't the type who would intentionally conduct criminal activities, but it was early March and he needed money. So long as he could distribute the joints without having to collect any money for the orders, he was willing to help. It was easier for me to keep him out of trouble that way.

On the west end of the park, you could always find me sitting on a bench, taking donations for peppermint candy in a small bucket. Everyone donating knew what the joint cost—like a five-dollar minimum donation. The peppermint candy would be a tradeoff for the joints Moke kept on the east side of the park. The peppermint stick exchanged for your five dollars would be removed from its wrapper and placed in a box sitting on the bench next to Moke. In return, he would place the very thin joint inside the wrapper and then pass it back to you. He was fine doing this with the understanding that he wasn't selling anything directly. All the students knew we had the good weed, as long as you had the right peppermint stick. Plus, the word was getting out. The problem was trying to sell weed to others who we didn't know, mainly because of my refusal to directly sell to anyone. Because of that, I would pass on making the extra cash. It wasn't worth the trouble of getting caught. Still, at the end of the day, the split from the peppermint bucket could easily amount to several hundred bucks.

***

Time was passing, and things were going really well in New York for the two of us until one really stormy day. While waiting for the train to arrive, I was standing inside a phone booth on a street corner talking to Lola. With thunder rumbling the walls and a heavy downpour of rain drenching the roof, I did my best to listen to her quavering voice as she tried to explain through the staticky phone that she had lost our child.

With that statement, I suddenly paused and asked, "How are you?"

She claimed she was doing better and was much healthier, but the pregnancy was seriously rough on her. After hearing what she said, I was left with a feeling of guilt. Undoubtedly, she needed my support, and I wasn't there for her. However, before hanging up, I promised her without a doubt that when my schooling was done, I would return for her.

But at that time, my focus was entirely wrapped around completing what I had set out to do—learn as much as possible about surveillance, security, and whatever else was covered under investigations. My motive was to think and perform the same as a detective. Staying one step ahead was important to me. If not, I wouldn't be of use to Lola or anyone else around me.

I had promised her upon completion of her last semester we would pack up and move to Flint, and that move was getting close. I couldn't see leaving her in such discomfort, especially having already failed her during the pregnancy. My promise was my bond, and the trip to Flint would be granted. Even if we had no place to live, it was somewhat reassuring that my older sister would provide room for us.

Chapter 20. Karol and Her Maturity

I had taken to coming home late after visiting Moke in Brooklyn to count what we had made from our daily activities, something I did nearly every evening after class. You could say it seemed as though I had started to mistreat Karol and my son while living together. The relationship had gone fairly well between the two of us, but lately things had begun to change, and not for the best. She wasn't the type to complain or fuss about anything, though she could tell within the last month my actions weren't the same. I started to consume more and more of the powerful TAC, even after promising myself to cut back. She wanted to see me do well in New York, as I had already once refused her help in getting me to attend college with her at Grambling State. New York wasn't any different for Karol, she was still trying everything within her power to get through to me, but it wasn't working. My mind was set when I came to New York, and no matter what she tried, it wasn't working. There were other things on my mind.

Still, we had a mutual understanding and respected each other, and wisely so. DeVaan was our only true connection. Staying there in New York was something I'd never intended on doing, and telling Karol... it just didn't come easy. Yet, I could sense that she knew. Unbeknownst to me, she, too, had begun to make plans to leave New York.

I met Karol in 1968, my junior year in high school. Even though we were at two different schools, she had something special that placed her above all others I had met. I first noticed her at a high school football game, cheering for her team as a member of the varsity booster squad. I turned to my friend J. Mac and asked, "Who's that?"

"Where?" he asked.

"The chick. First row, second from the end. Who's that?"

"That's Karol. She's talking to Jimmy, and everybody's afraid to say anything to her."

"Why?"

"Because he's a bully, and he runs everyone off who tries."

"Can you introduce us?"

"Yeah, that's no problem. Her best friend is someone I know."

"Who's her best friend?"

"You know those triplets? Their sister."

"Hot? From across the track? You know Hot?"

"Yeah! The shortstop on our baseball team is my friend too, and he's been trying hard to get with her. Heck, man, it shouldn't be a problem because we're always around her."

Hot was beautiful. Though short in stature, she was incredibly built, with a bright complexion, pretty brown eyes, and gorgeous long hair.

"A'right, J. Mac. In that case, when can you do it?"

"Sometime this week. Is that okay?"

"Sure, that-ta be fine."

***

Their next game was homecoming, and I needed him to introduce us before then, which he did. The fact that we were at two different schools didn't bother me. I would drive from our predominantly White school, which sat on the north end of town, to our all-Black school at the extreme southwest end just to walk Karol and her sisters back across the railroad tracks to their house.

After walking them home from school several times, Jimmy, who was very violent and overpowering, got word of it. He then sent word by one of his boys to let me know if I kept walking them home, he would meet me on top of the railroad tracks up past Ms. Matthews's house and kick my a**.

***

Let's pause for a second right here and acknowledge Ms. Matthews as this scene takes place. In the year 1968, Ms. Matthews was 55 years of age. This incident took place exactly 55 years ago, and most importantly, the scene is being written 55 years later. If it's God's will, Ms. Matthews will be 110 years of age when this story is published. Kudos to Ms. Matthews for such longevity in life.

***

After receiving his message, I didn't walk them every evening, but I didn't stop doing it, either. One particular day, I decided to walk with them. Full of joy after leaving their house and on my way back to my grandmother's café where I kept my car, I found Jimmy standing there waiting for me with his crew. He really wasn't expecting me to show up, surely not by myself, but being raised on the back side of Fourth Street meant remembering one thing in life—it's not whether you win or lose a fight, but having the courage to show up.

What Jimmy failed to realize was, I wasn't alone. After he sent the message to me, I decided to have my best friend drive my car on those days I walked with them. He'd wait for me just north of Ms. Matthews's house. You couldn't help but wave at Ms. Matthews as she sat on her front porch watching as you passed by. Every time I walked them to their house across the bayou, my friend would park just north of her house and wait. You could see the car, sitting not far from the sawdust burning pile on the other end of the railroad tracks, which gave me the courage to not worry about getting jumped.

My friends knew Jimmy was waiting before I did, and as I approached the railroad tracks, I could see all of them, both groups standing near the pile of sawdust, arguing back and forth about what

122

would happen once I showed up. With Jimmy being the bully he was, the argument was sure to escalate.

I didn't give a damn about fighting. It was something we did all the time in the alley where I was raised in back of Haney's Big House nightclub and Bob Taylor's gambling shack. Upon my arrival, the argument switched to him and me facing off next to the burning pile of sawdust, fed by an overhead conveyor belt from the sawmill. I had planned a strategy while everyone else was arguing, but I couldn't wrap my mind around any of this because Karol had never mentioned one thing about her and him the whole time I had been walking her home.

I didn't know Jimmy, which didn't mean anything, but if there was something else he had against me that I couldn't envision, then now was the time to find out. My plan was to get as close to the burning pile as possible. If he was really tough and not just a bully, then it wouldn't matter where this fight took place. I moved even closer to the pile while we argued, hoping it would put fear in whatever he was thinking about doing to me. Dammit, I was fed up with him. My anxiety had turned into pure anger. I wasn't backing down, and if there was going to be a fight, I was making darn sure it would be one hot sawdust fight.

Finally, after arguing back and forth for way too long, he decided to give me a pass, letting me know I needed to get the hell out of there. I wasn't sure what it was that worked in my favor—my bluff to fight in the hot ashes or my friends showing up to even things out. (Lesson learned—never ignore a threatening message. Get help. It might save your life.)

A few months into our relationship, we were informed that Jimmy had gotten involved in a more serious triangle and was eventually killed. Karol and I did what we thought was right—we met at the church to attend his funeral. By the way, it wasn't Karol whom he had been dating when I met her. It turns out he just didn't want me coming across the tracks into his neighborhood.

Meanwhile, I was trying to secure a relationship with a person who I had not yet realized was one of the smartest people at her school. It was a struggle at first, trying to convince Karol to at least give me an opportunity to come inside to meet her parents. All she talked about was school, studying, and grades. My grades, on the other hand, were dreadfully low, and it seemed my chances of her accepting me to come study with her were even lower. I was having a hard time in my predominantly White school, and I spent most of it trying to protect whomever I could from danger. With only 5 percent Black students, I had taken it upon myself to see that they were getting to class safely, so most of the time I would be late for class. Sometimes I wouldn't make it to class at all. The things that were done to some of those students were awful, and being protected while there was a must. Heck, my little gang, the Demons, didn't mind coming to help. None gave a darn about studying, nor did they care about attending school all day, either.

However, Karol felt I could do better with my time. She promised if I could bring my grades up by midterm, when my junior prom rolled around, there would be a great possibility she would attend it with me. Heck! I had no idea how I could manage that. I never had a study method of any kind and never earned a grade higher than a C. But if I wanted to be with her and still be the leader of our little Demon gang, I had to change, and I had to do it fast.

To keep all the guys thinking I was still one who didn't give a damn about anything and had no reason to study for school, I had to come up with a plan. Now don't get me wrong—some or most of the guys were smart, a lot sharper than I was, but they were being misled.

What could I do? I thought. Well, my decision was to leave all copies of my original issued books in my hall locker. Then I would *steal* another set of the same books and keep them at home to study with. Therefore, things would look normal to the fellows, like I had no interest in studying because they would never see me with a book of any kind in my hands. Of course, I had to start attending class regularly. That meant less protection for the Black students, but considering Karol's ultimatum and realizing it was the only way I could be with her, I started to strive for excellence. Every evening after school when I got home, I couldn't wait to dive into my homework. I still struggled with some of my subjects, like biology and even English, for that matter, but even those grades improved to a D.

After stopping the guys from coming on campus and giving myself time to study, things got worse for the Black students. They were being attacked. One of them, Clearance, who was among the smarter students, was punched in the face. If it hadn't been for Hester, who was in English class with the two of us and let me know what happened, it would have slipped completely by us. Clearance asked that nothing physically happen to the guy, and we honored that request, but we did scare the living heck out of him.

After midterm, Karol and I started seeing more of each other, and when the time came for prom night, I was ready and sporting something different—a pair of starched blue jean coveralls, with a crease in the legs that could nearly stand on its own, a gold long-sleeved shirt topped with a lavender necktie, and a gold-colored Stetson hat. Karol was traditionally dressed in a charming evening gown, with the prettiest set of earrings that sparkled brightly. I watched as she dazzled everyone in her beautiful prom outfit, and best of all, we had a marvelous time together.

Huh! Speaking of having a marvelous time—we did, but maybe too good of a time. I had promised everyone I would have her home by midnight, and that I did, but not before we stopped for a passionate coital encounter. It was our first real date, our first time being intimate, and I never gave it a thought that she would become pregnant. Yes, Karol became pregnant after the very first time we were sexually involved. I was young, she was even younger, and we didn't have a clue what to do once we found out. Luckily, we had a great supporting cast—my mother and, of course, my father, who had just been released from prison for the last time in January, 1970, the same year DeVaan was born. She also had her parents and a host of sisters who were willing to pitch in to help.

Most of all, Karol had herself. She knew exactly what she wanted, and she went after it with strong desire and willing determination. After the baby was born and school was out, I left for Michigan, and she went on to finish high school. By 1976, she was a college graduate.

After college, she moved to Queens, New York, accepting a job as a bank auditor for Bankers Trust in downtown Manhattan. As for me, I took a very different route to get there, but nonetheless, I finally moved to New York, maybe not for the right reasons or even for the reason Karol had hoped, but for whatever reason, I was there with the two of them. The problem was, I wasn't sure if the person who was there with them was any stronger or better as a family man than the one who left them in Louisiana in the beginning. And, of course, after she and I had spent a couple of months together, she began to accept that about me.

Obviously, the person I'd become wasn't the person she once knew, and it wasn't for the best. Karol knew I couldn't accomplish all the things I was doing unless I had some type of hustle. Time was passing, and she'd noticed not once had there ever been an attempt by me to at least look for a job. Yet she observed me purchasing excessive amounts of gas and paying tolls as I ran all around the city, not coming in until at least midnight but most nights closer to 1:00 a.m., never explaining where I'd been or what I'd been doing.

Even though she sensed that something was terribly wrong, she never interrupted my stay or my opportunity to attend and finish school. Never once did she harass me about my late nights or why I wasn't spending time with my son. She just accepted my actions and went ahead with her own plans, which involved accepting a job in Los Angeles and taking our son with her.

She had a small hope that someday I would change, and we could finally become a real family. By the time she realized I wasn't ready, we had truly grown apart, and she had become successful, accomplishing great things as she finally moved on with her life.

Chapter 21. Modeling Instructor's Troubles

"Mr. Lamond" was how Ms. Kourtney Lockhart from the modeling school addressed me. There was something distinct about Ms. Lockhart that made talking with her come easy. She would sit with me after our modeling sessions most evenings, telling fascinating stories about some of the most famous and extraordinary English attractions, such as the Tower of London, Westminster Abbey, and Windermere, where you could take a cruise and view the beauty of Britain's largest natural lake. Her stories were so vivid, they were like an actual guided tour. She brought the scenery so close, it seemed almost visible.

Ms. Lockhart had other stories as well that she would share with me. All types of tragic New York City stories and listening to her would be like your big sister reading a bedtime story at night from a storybook. Ms. Lockhart was from the UK, the greater London area, and she strived to become a screenwriter and director. She was a very beautiful person whose job was to teach runway-style techniques and pre-acting classes.

I was the first student to enter her class that evening, and I took a seat up front. "Ms. Lockhart?"

"Yes?" She turned to me.

"I'm curious—would you mind if I was to ask you something personal?"

"Only if you're not getting out of line, Mr. Lamond. Yes, you may."

Since we were in her classroom all alone, her statement was understandable. "No, that would never happen, but we've been having these after-class conversations for quite a while now... why does everyone call you Ms. Lockhart? Aren't you guys married? Why haven't you changed your name?"

"Inquiring mind, Mr. Lamond... and definitely it's not out of line. Frankly, to tell you the truth—that has been a controversial decision of mine, one my husband has questioned me about for years."

"Why haven't you?" I pried.

"Mr. Lamond, your curiosity is surprising. Why are you concerned if I may ask?"

"Only because when school first started, I would watch you and your husband leave for lunch a few times, and the surname on his company's name tag hanging from his lanyard happened to be different. And once I noticed that, it's always been something of interest to me. From what I've heard, over ninety percent of European women most commonly change their names to their husbands.'"

"Amazing that you noticed and took an interest, Mr. Lamond, but no problem. It's only for professional status. We do legally share the same name."

"Okay, Ms. Lockhart, do you guys have any children?"

"No, we don't! However, one day I would love to, and speaking of children—in one of our previous conversations you mentioned you have a son. Does he have your last name?" I was shocked she asked. I had never been asked about my son before, and I didn't know how to respond.

I wasn't spending much time with him, either. I wanted to, but this "It" that was driving me wasn't allowing for that. "No, he doesn't, I'm sorry to say. When he was born, we were young and unmarried. That left me with a clear understanding of why my last name wasn't given to him. Still, I was a bit surprised and dejected after finding out he had neither my first Vincentius nor my last Lamond."

"Do you think the fact he wasn't named after you could be affecting your relationship?"

"It could have some effect, but a name... could it possibly have that much effect on how I feel about her?"

"I can't tell you that. You'll have to dig deep into your inner self to find out, but you must in order to make things work with her."

"Wow! You may be right, but to repair my inner self, I'm not sure if I have enough time left here in New York to even focus on accomplishing that. Maybe there is something Ms. Lockhart, about her, deep within that keeps me at a distance, but I'm not sure if it's something I really want to know. Some things are better left undone... I've been granted an opportunity, Ms. Lockhart, and mending my inner self to salvage our relationship is not why I'm here, though it has been a pleasure to share time with her and my son."

"Then why *are* you here?"

"Honestly, Ms. Lockhart, to attend school. That's why I'm here at Barbizon, to learn fashion and gain physical coordination, to be able to use my hands gracefully and with speed, and to perform and act appropriately for any occasion that arises. Being able to outwit and deceive others has always been a burning desire of mine. And as for the other school, it's the one thing that brought me to New York in the first place, not Karol and my son, though I'm not saying that I don't love them, because I do, but they just happened to be living here. And when I leave New York, the schools will have taught me things that I need, things like how to think, act, and perform like a detective."

"A detective, you said. Is that the other school you're attending?"

"Yes! And I love it, Ms. Lockhart. I have to be able to stay a step or two ahead of the law, and I must look the part while I do it."

"Hmm... A professional model slash private eye. That's pretty intriguing, Mr. Lamond. A devilishly handsome guy isn't usually running around doing dirty work for others. Those are two extremely conflicting professions, but it's very fascinating, to say the least."

She appeared to be enjoying our conversations, forming something of an interest in the progress being made in my life. She would always encourage me to continue my good work, leaving me to think there was some type of genuine bond between the two of us. But no, there wasn't one. Once the investigative school came to her attention, it was only then Ms. Lockhart started to take more interest in me. I didn't realize the reason at first, but eventually I would. I was about to become a private investigator, a graduate of one of the most successful private investigation and security schools in the country. My graduation from modeling school was near as well. She was starting to figure out how I could be an asset to her.

A couple of weeks came and went, and she began to get closer to me as if she were really interested in my wellbeing. The reason for it dawned on me not long after hearing the tales Ms. Lockhart shared with me about her husband. I discerned later her motive for gaining my trust—she saw me as someone who could help in finding out what was up with her husband. Clearly, she could tell something wasn't right, stating his evenings away from home had gotten to be unbearable. Rarely would he get home before 10:30 p.m., and sometimes as late as midnight. He wouldn't say anything—just shower and go to bed. We both could relate to that, as I was having my own issues staying out late and not doing right by Karol and my son. Yet, I would sit and listen while she poured her heart out.

A year prior to my enrollment, she had sent for her cousin to come live with them. Oftentimes, her husband would be working late, finalizing real estate deals, and the loneliness had started to overwhelm her. The cousin had moved on by the time I showed up, and around the same time, Ms. Lockhart began suspecting that John Paul, a renowned realtor, had started cheating on her. Whether it was with the cousin or with others, she wasn't sure. She had no proof, just suspicion and hearsay.

I gathered from most of her conversations that she was saddened by his actions and needed to know more about his gradual changes over the last year. I felt sorry for Ms. Lockhart, and I asked if I could do anything for her, however, I wasn't sure if I could do anything at all. It sure sounded like she could use some help, and I was energetic and eager to give my investigative skills a try. She accepted and gave me her cousin's home address and her husband's work address and phone number. This information was more than enough to get me started on my first case.

Chapter 22. Checking Their Personal Moves

It was Monday, April 18, 1977. Clouds were lingering over the city, but the sun was trying to peek through and make it a sunny morning. The weather was beginning to change. People were up early. Dogs were wagging their tails and barking excitedly. Everyone was walking with a smile but still not speaking to each other. Remember, it was New York City, where one must accept whatever kindness an individual offers.

We had been in school now for nearly three months. As I entered through the investigation school's double doors, Juncos was the first to greet me in the lobby that morning.

"Vincent! You ready for the school's investigative street tour at the end of the month?"

"I'm not sure about the tour, Juncos. However, I've been told it's an exciting event."

"Yeah, Vincent! It is. Plus, you'll finally get a chance to holler at Ariana. She's been dying to meet you."

Ariana was Juncos's sister, who happened to work for a bank in downtown Manhattan. He had made significant efforts to get Ariana and me together, but my suspicion of him kept me avoiding any of his proposals. However, that was tough to accomplish, seeing that we were classmates, and his persistence only increased.

Nonetheless, I continued to resist, especially after learning from Newt that Juncos's distribution class in Saint Louis was fake. That increased my suspicion of him, on top of our living in the same apartment complex and attending the same damn school.

Juncos had worked under my leadership at our job in Oklahoma. Now he appeared to have been assigned the task of gathering information on me. The problem was, he wasn't gaining ground, nor had he gathered enough information to start any type of interrogation. I gathered from Newt the office he was sent from was about to pull the plug on him.

"What do you mean? How will your sister and I get a chance to meet if there's a scheduled itinerary for this field trip?" He then went on to explain the bank where his sister worked was on our list of places to visit.

From my understanding, the field trip would be very entertaining, with the instructors giving each student a different assignment to perform while walking the busy streets of Manhattan. Others would be assigned tasks to complete as if they were civilian shoppers, some having special surveillance to cover.

Getting a chance to holler at Juncos's sister wasn't an issue because she was the bank's lead loan officer. The school and the bank were in an agreement that students should be allowed to enter and be shown particular investigative jobs of interest, jobs affiliated with banks that might be available to them once they graduated. One other student and I were given this assignment, with a chance to listen to Ariana give a lecture about banks and their security assignments.

Whatever they were throwing at me, whether it was Juncos's sister or the bank itself, I wasn't interested. My time left at school was limited, and getting my diploma and getting the hell out of the city were paramount to me.

A week passed before that Monday morning the 18th, and I'd spent most of it covering Ms. Lockhart's husband. She had given me his personal information earlier, along with her cousin's. Tracking him down, covering a few of his home and business real estate showings, as well as following her cousin back and forth from work, kept me occupied and exhausted.

After leaving the investigative school and arriving at the evening's modeling session, the same day, I approached Ms. Lockhart. It was later that same evening the eighteenth, and I was still tired from the strenuous week I had investigating Ms. Lockhart's husband and her cousin.

"Hey, Ms. Lockhart, is there someplace we could meet other than the usual spot here at school?"

"Sure. Would you care for a cocktail?"

"Heck, Ms. Lockhart, we both could probably use a mild sedative. A double shot of Henny wouldn't hurt. What time, and where do you have in mind?"

"Nine o'clock after the last runway session. There's a nice little pub down on Queens Boulevard and Sixty-Third. It's less than a five-minute drive, within walking distance, actually, right here in Rego Park. Occasionally, our faculty gathers there, and sometimes students as well, so no suspicion will be raised if we're seen there together. What do you think? Can you make it?"

Noticing Ms. Lockhart could barely squeeze her statement out, seriously hurting from not knowing what her husband was up to, I had to agree. She was willing to find out at any cost. Her desire to know what her husband was doing was burning so hot she could no longer stand it.

"I think it's cool, and don't worry, I'll find the place."

I had already spent several hours working between both schools and anticipated more long hours over the weekend following both Ms. Lockhart's cousin, Mina, and her husband, John Paul. Never once could I place the two of them together. Seriously, there was a need to meet with Ms. Lockhart specifically to share what information I did have, which really wasn't much at all.

I'd researched John Paul's real estate listings for homes and condos in the area, thinking I could convince him I was interested in buying. After watching his movements from the homes he showed, I needed to see what was going on inside. The only way that could be done was to have a session with him. Once I gathered all the necessary information, setting up a meeting with him was pressing.

Later that night, I joined Ms. Lockhart at the bar, which was relatively easy to find. "Mr. Lamond, I see that you've made it, and on time."

She seemed more relaxed and back to normal—probably from the hope of getting some encouraging news. What a disappointment the meeting would be for her. John Paul's inside movements were still unknown, and the thought crossed my mind to spin his movements into something more positive for her.

"Ms. Lockhart, before we get started, I must ask—are you sure you'd like to continue with this investigation on your husband? Because he doesn't look to be doing much other than working a lot of long hours."

"Are you positive?"

"No, I'm not. However, there is one thing I'd like to be sure of, but you must be prepared for any future findings if there's anything to it."

"Don't tell me he's cheating, Vincent!"

"I'm not sure, but that's the reason we're here, isn't it? To construct a plan to observe what your husband is really doing?"

"Yes, you have a point."

"Then are you prepared? Because I do have a plan."

"Yes! I've worried and been lonely for far too long. Let's do it!"

"Okay! First, we need to come up with a plan to disguise my appearance. If your husband were to come by the school, we wouldn't want him noticing me."

"True, a disguise would be smart. I doubt John would show up, though. He hasn't been by the school for some time now."

"Ms. Lockhart, you can never be too sure of anything."

She was only looking at things from her point of view—that her husband was never around. For me, it was my job to find out why, and most of all to keep my identity unknown. Indeed, if this was going to take place, and if I was going to pull it off, then he had to be seriously misled. I was left with the job of constructing a very careful plan to find out what John Paul was really up to.

"Ms. Lockhart, how's your drink?"

"The drink is fine, can't you tell?" We both giggled.

"Yes! Maybe your fourth should be without alcohol."

"You think?"

"Yes. If not, I'll have to carry your butt out of here."

"Don't worry, I got this. Now, continue with your plan."

"Okay! Ms. Lockhart, to keep your husband from noticing me, my appearance would have to be camouflaged, let's talk disguises."

"All right, Lamond. I'm willing to pay for all disguises and any tools you need."

"In that case, I'll need a hairpiece."

"What about a toupee?"

"A what? Come on, Ms. Lockhart. Me rocking a toupee? This is the seventies."

"Okay, then what do you suggest?"

"A large Afro hair weave would be perfect, and there's a little boutique down on Astoria Boulevard in East Elmhurst where I can get any type of weave that looks natural on me."

"Fine! If that's what you want, then let's get it done. Get whatever you need and check back with me later."

She seemed more energized after our meeting, and hearing her husband may not have been doing anything wrong could have been the reason. It had gotten late. We'd both had more than enough to drink, and our words started to slur. Plus, she had begun to drop the prefix from my name.

"Ms. Lockhart, do you need a ride home?"

"I'll be fine, Lamond. My vehicle's right out front."

Chapter 23. Real Estate Showings

It didn't take long to rule out the cousin, Mina. Following her around for a few days revealed she had a steady male friend visiting her. That left me able to focus on what John Paul was up to.

There was this cosmetology boutique specializing in hair mods, from Bob Marley dreadlocks to modern-day African American Afros. The weave would complete the transformation to my new identity. Hell, modeling school wasn't only teaching us how to walk the runway with style. Makeup and acting classes were a huge part of the school's curriculum, and that came in handy.

My plan was to get John Paul to meet with me at one of his home shows, and he agreed to meet me in two weeks on Friday, May 6. That would give me the opportunity to focus on gaining his interest in meeting me for a second visit. The initial meeting would also allow me to scope area listings for the Queens homes that were featured in his catalog. Most importantly, I'd be driving myself to the home showings in the Monte Carlo, eliminating the use of any public transportation and making it easier and more efficient to move around.

John Paul arrived at our first house showing with a female business assistant, an agent in training, I was told. After everyone had gone and the showing was complete, the agent and John Paul remained inside. It was something he had done in a previous showing with a different female agent, which left me suspicious. Actually, I didn't see them fooling around, but as they stepped outside, the way they held hands—both hands in front of one another, with him pulling her into a loving embrace—was enough to give me an idea that something was going on, even if I wasn't sure of myself.

The next showing would be several days later at one of John Paul's condo listings, and before our scheduled appointment, it was crucial for me to make an unannounced visit. One done all alone, giving me the opportunity to assess the property and create easy access for Moke whenever he was ready to enter. Moke had to be in place before John or I were set to arrive.

This place, an unoccupied, two-story condominium, was beautiful! I was impressed standing before its luxurious English-style façade. Someone looked to have spent a great deal of time designing its luxury features, but despite that, way too little time was spent on its locking devices. They were more like art exhibits than actual functioning locks. Entering into the condo would be simple, and I'd get the chance once again to use my locksmithing tools.

Something about the thrill of doing wrong ignited my persona. I stood there thinking, *Should I or should I not do this?* knowing all along breaking and entering was wrong and unethical, even if the condo wasn't in use.

It had to be Satan emerging in me, bringing out this "It" from within, and there wasn't a damn thing I could do about it. There I was, standing before these two beautiful, extremely large double doors, grasping for what little control of righteousness I could muster and trying to submerge this "It" that just wouldn't go away. It was like fighting a shadow, something you can see but not grab or make go away.

Shit! I thought. *These doors have to be the most ravishing and elegant doors I've ever seen.* I found myself shaking my head, wasting time admiring their elegance. I didn't have time for this, so I pulled my most commonly used tool from my pouch. With it, I proceeded to pick the lock of the right door. The front of the house was the most exposed area, but it was the easiest and the quickest to pick considering the back entrance was protected by two doors, one inner and one outer that was mounted on a steel frame and secured with a pair of deadbolts.

After stepping inside, beholding the huge size of the home gave me an idea that would give me an advantage that I could use to control the outcome of our next visit. Because of its enormous size, I could now show an extreme lack of interest, claiming there wasn't a need for me to further view the entire home, which was too large for a single person. That would make it all the safer for Moke as well, to maneuver around inside and find out what actually went on after a client left the premises.

With that thought in mind and realizing what was left to do, I continued to look around while making my way to unlock the back doors, leaving Moke with no problem gaining access. The showing wasn't an open house, therefore the chances of any other clients showing up would be minimal to none, making things that much safer for Moke once he was inside.

My major concern was keeping the area chosen for him to settle into free and clear of traffic. With that covered, after leaving the premises under the assumption the condo was too large for me, I could only hope luring John Paul to the home would be enough for him to engage in his usual activities.

Departing the premises was taking a chance, but to stay would be more of a challenge and putting Moke at risk of getting caught, knowing he would already be inside before anyone else arrived. I had no knowledge of what agents did when a home showing was completed, but what John Paul was doing seemed very strange and inappropriate to me.

The day had come, Saturday, May 14. It was overcast, and the dense clouds brought with them a hint of misty rain. In spite of the weather, it was still a fine day for a home showing. As planned earlier, Moke had already positioned himself inside and out of everyone's way.

I wasn't sure if anyone else had shown up yet, but my approach to the extraordinary condo was very tentative. Finally, I strolled up the walkway, cleared the two steps to a beautiful set of French doors, and pulled the gold chain. A beautiful melody sounded from directly above the double doors. I stood there mystified, as it seemed for some reason to ring for an exceedingly long time.

I waited until a door suddenly opened. There stood a guy, though it wasn't John Paul.

"Hello, you must be Mr. Vaughn?"

"Yes!"

"Please, come in."

"Thank you."

"Mr. Vaughn, how are you? We're glad you could make it. My name is Jacob, John's assistant. Come, let me show you around."

"Wow, this place is enormous!" I said after stepping inside. "Too large."

"You don't like it, Mr. Vaughn?"

"No, that isn't it at all, Jacob," I said, looking up at the high, arched ceiling, both palms held upward, gesturing at the beauty of the condo. "Actually, I love the home, but it's extremely huge... I'm sorry, but this is way too much for me. Is there something smaller you could show me?"

"Are you sure? Would you care to look around?"

"No, my mind is made up. We should have discussed the square footage of this condo beforehand. Is John Paul here?"

"Sure! He's upstairs. Please wait. I'll be back shortly."

My job was done, and that was to get John Paul to the home, mostly to see if another female agent would be accompanying him. There wasn't one, and my theory of something going on after his home showings had failed. Overwhelmed by my disappointment, all I could do was wait for Jacob's return with John Paul, give him a generous handshake and a short conversation, and exit the premises. Unbeknownst to John, I was waiting for him in the disguise of Mr. Vaughn, and it was time for Mr. Vaughn to dislodge himself from the showing.

"John, this is way too huge for me. I'm sorry for any inconvenience I may have caused. Like I told your assistant Jacob, the square footage of this condo should have been discussed. I'm sorry, but you'll have to find me something a bit smaller."

"I understand, Mr. Vaughn and getting you something smaller will be a priority of mine."

"Great. You have my number. I'll be looking for your call."

They seemed a little displeased but overall, not too concerned about my decision to leave. I left through the front entrance with a great feeling of self-satisfaction that the agents showed no sign there could have been someone else in the home. On the other hand, my theory about John Paul being involved with a female assistant being wrong left me very disgruntled.

Still, John Paul and his assistant Jacob did indeed stay at the condo, as I had hoped. With that happening, my impression of everything changed. Was this something normal that happened all the time with agents and their assistants? With a *guy* assisting John, my entire theory of his cheating went completely out of the window.

I kept thinking, though—*What was he really up to?* Could he be dealing in something illegal? I left confused and wondering if I had put Moke in some type of danger. I wanted to return, but what could I do? *It was only a house showing that didn't take place,* I told myself.

However, I decided to give it some time. I waited up the street to see if someone else would show up, but nothing happened. My presence was needed elsewhere. With no idea how long John Paul would be inside, I left. Everything was up to Moke now.

It turned out more than an hour had passed before he was able to leave the condo and catch the train back to Brooklyn, but not before he acquired something useful.

Moke had taken photos, but with the development process taking several days, he could not produce proof of what he had obtained, and that left all interested parties in suspense. After finding out what Moke had, would Ms. Lockhart be willing to accept it and fight to keep her marriage intact? She was truly lonely, yet she was in love with her husband and wanted their marriage to work.

Gosh! What an effort I had put into researching Ms. Lockhart's situation, too much and oh boy, it caused me to forget that May was a special month—the month of Lola's birthday. As if things were not already bad enough, I wasn't keeping in touch as I should have. To strengthen her belief that I was returning for her, something had to be done differently, especially if I were to keep her interested in traveling to Flint, Michigan, with me. Whether she was losing interest or not, I didn't know. What I did know, however, was I would be finishing both schools in July.

After that, I could get back to Sonny about his warehouse assortment of machine guns and ammunition. I needed to know if they were still available. To my understanding, twenty had already been removed from inventory, with Sonny explaining he had disassembled and prepared them for shipment.

Our initial conversation hadn't allowed for any discussion of what type or brand they were, but I had faith in Sonny and believed the weapons would be good to reassemble for street sale. Sonny was my homeboy from nearby Monroe, Louisiana, and with all our previous jobs having gone well, I had no reason not to believe in him. His bills of lading were in numerical sequence, and acquiring fake copies to ship some scrap dunnage in place of the guns was nearly impossible for him. His reasoning for striking up that conversation in the first place was my expertise in producing an authentic carrier's copy. Actually, the ammo and artillery to him were no good without an authentic-looking duplicate. There was no way his original numerical copy could be shipped with several pallets of rejected cargo. Therefore, when I was done in New York, I would contact him. I anticipated making several thousand dollars while waiting for Lola.

Chapter 24. Tracking Postal Money Orders

The weekend was over. It was Monday, the twenty-third of May, 1977. Fatigue had begun to settle all over my body. Nearly half the year had gone by before the first news broadcast about the illegal cashing of the money orders. One of New York's local TV stations announced the feds were close to tracking down those responsible.

From the composite of information gathered, and with the number of ID cards used, the feds had concluded it was more than a one-man operation. Among their findings, they determined the first money order cashed had originated in one of the upper Manhattan area Banks. From my understanding, they were pinning it on a gang leader who was residing in the New York-New Jersey area.

I had reassured myself the time spent planning the job was thorough enough that it should have gone undetected. But no, there hadn't been enough planning, and it didn't throw them off completely! They were on to a group, but how close were they?

I didn't realize the heavy consumption of drugs could have been causing my mind to have an inability to fully concentrate, which left me pondering how to keep the feds thrown off. That normally wouldn't have been a problem for me. Usually, I would go over my plan several times back and forth before taking any action. Looking back, I hadn't done my normal amount of preparation, and after cashing them, I never gave the money orders another thought. That was very unlike me, and I knew it. Now I felt I needed to make a deep commitment and exercise my inner strength. That, combined with my faith, would allow me to overcome what I thought was causing my problem.

Even with the money orders being well documented with double IDs, very little thought process had gone into the plan itself.

Without my usual run-through and thorough preparation, the scheme was in a vulnerable situation that put my whole life in jeopardy, especially with the lack of knowledge that the feds and other government officials were paying close attention to me. They all were aware of my move to New York, and that gave them deep concern since everything happened within the first month of my visit, increasing the possibility in their eyes that my involvement with the group was probable. More often than not, my movements would be much sharper than those of the cops, but my sedative slowdowns while under the influence of drugs gave the cops time to gain ground. Mentally, there was no way to fully concentrate on everything at hand. It was all a blur.

With the spiritual guidance instilled in me by my mother while growing up, I knew the drug was not part of this "It" I had no control over. With that said, there was no doubt I could overcome my drug use.

It was clear to me the news channel had been informed that some group was responsible for all the unauthorized money orders cashed in and around the city. If there *was* a group cashing illegal money orders, then I didn't know of it. That meant, messy as I had been, my plan had worked well enough to throw everyone off into thinking a group of individuals had cashed those money orders. Could there really have been a group that I knew nothing about?

Things had not been taken seriously enough, and Juncos was still working desperately on the scheduled field trip, which was approaching soon. This would happen on some of Manhattan's busiest streets, with an inside tour through one of New York's most prominent banks. I never considered this to be anything more than just a tour and a field trip. Surely it had nothing to do with the cashed money orders from months ago.

Normally, I would have been curious and deterred the field trip, but having the inability to fully think, it never bothered me. The downtown field trip was an isolated event away from the school, a normal part of its curriculum, I thought. And maybe it was, but it was also a good opportunity for Juncos to put something into play. He had to come up with a plan, and it had to be soon because graduation was near, and he was running out of time. He wasn't being paid just to have fun, and I wasn't making it easy for him to complete his assignment. With only a little over a month left in New York, keeping myself clean and staying clear of everyone was important.

Now with my thought process extremely clear, it was easy for me to reflect back. If the first money order was cashed in a bank in the upper Manhattan area, as the New York news broadcast had reported, then that wasn't one of mine.

It also became clear to me that the use of public transportation was making it easy for me to be followed. Juncos's presence had come to be annoying. Because of that, I pulled the damn Monte Carlo from the rooftop of the adjacent building and started using it, making it difficult for him to keep up. Not only did his annoying presence bother me, but his being the lead student in charge of our field trip had me unsettled as well. He didn't seem to be the type who should be in charge, and definitely not in charge of anything over me.

Yes! My mind was now clear, clear enough that it became obvious what he was up to, getting his sister and me together and claiming she really wanted to meet me. Whether she did or not, I couldn't know, but one thing was for sure—he needed me at that bank on this field trip. If the news station was aware of the money orders cashed in a bank in upper Manhattan so were the people who were trying to find out who did it. By the way, if they were looking for a certain signature of some type, or whatever Juncos had planned, I wasn't giving in to it. Plus, I'd never used a bank in no parts of New York to cash a money order.

Finally, the field trip was upon us. It had already been set back once before from its original date. As planned, Juncos's sister was there to greet us at the bank. It was Friday the twenty-seventh of May, and students were scattered all over the downtown area.

"Ariana, is it?"

"Yes! And you must be Vincent, right?"

"You mean he actually mentioned me?"

"Juan has spoken of you several times, but your name tag also gave you away. Is this the other student?"

"Yes."

"You must be Earl, the undergrad student. How're you?"

"I'm good, and I must say, it's a pleasure to be chosen as a participant. Hopefully, the tour is as exciting as you appear to be." We all smiled while sharing a little laughter.

"You wouldn't be flirting, would you, Earl?" she asked.

"No, never!"

"Great! Then it's a pleasure to meet you both. Here, Vincent, take these forms that we had you guys fill out a few weeks prior. You and your classmate look over them to verify the highlighted areas are correct and return them to me."

Although Ariana was Puerto Rican, she could pass for a Caucasian American, especially with her hazel-green eyes. She had a distinguished look, one that showed her in a professional and business-oriented way. Unlike her brother, she spoke in more of a standard New Yorker accent. To look at them both, they shared no resemblance, but who was I to judge? At least Juncos had one thing right—she had my interest. She worked for a bank.

After we both verified the highlighted information and returned the questionnaires, we were eligible to continue with the tour. I hadn't been clear on how many security jobs there were within the banking industry, some obvious and others___ one would never think of, from uniformed policemen to plainclothes cops to interior investigative loan officers working undercover. The tour was enthralling. To call it intriguing would be an understatement, but why me? I couldn't understand why Juncos had chosen me for the bank tour unless he had something planned with his sister. All along, I'd been suspicious of Juncos. It all seemed like a trap, one that held several similarities to the previous bank my ex-wife had worked for. She was being pressured into trapping me into an atrocious web that would have been nearly impossible to escape.

It was very smart of him, knowing it would be almost impossible for me to resist any banking scheme, especially if there was some inside help to pull it off. What Juan didn't realize was I knew why he was in New York, and I was refusing to be cornered by any of his plans. With that in mind, as long as I could keep him off schedule and unaware that I was onto his undercover scheming, I had an advantage over him.

As the tour progressed, time didn't present a chance to hold a long conversation with Ariana. We spent most of our visit in areas that were guarded, either by security guards, uniformed policemen, or plainclothesmen. For the bank to agree and grant such an exclusive inside visit was beyond belief. Never did it register with me that it was a true part of the school's curriculum, but it was. The bank had an agreement with the school to present an annual downtown field trip. A couple of students would be chosen to tour one of Manhattan's most prominent banks, with the goal of intriguing them into taking positions with certain agents in bank protection. But why choose me? Why would I be shown some of the most secure areas of the bank? If Juncos had been assigned to follow me, he must have had a reason for choosing me as one of the students for the bank tour.

"Shit!" I muttered. *Maybe it's another one of my paranoid moments.* My mind wandered, and then I had a flashback. Just a few months ago, I had driven up and down the entire East Coast, cashing money orders. Today, I'd been given a chance to visit the inside of an affiliate bank, one of the banks it was believed a money order could have landed. What were the odds of that?

Man! I thought. *The two of them must have a plan. Being exposed to these private areas of the bank was intriguing, tempting, and very attractive to someone like me. What if though, there was a way, without getting caught, I could convince her to reverse whatever plan they had, and she and I alone were to swindle what we could out of this bank? Heck, should I get deeper into her?*

"Ariana, does working here ever ruffle your nerve that something could happen unexpectedly?"

"Not really, Vincent. There's always a sufficient amount of security in the building, even if you don't recognize who and where they are."

"Hey, since Earl has left for the men's room and we're here alone having this one-on-one conversation, I'm just curious—what if that unexpected thing wasn't caused by physical force? Then what?"

"Why, Vincent? Why would you inquire about that? And what do you mean if it 'wasn't caused by physical force'?" She spoke quietly and looked around, scratching the right side of her cheek with the tip of her index fingernail.

"Ariana, you never had a thought of an inside job? People are always inquisitive when a great deal of money is involved. What about your unrecognizable security would it be effective in stopping something like that?"

"Holy... Vincent, I must say—this is a very unusual conversation, and your curiosity is quite unexpected. But to answer your question, I would say trying to stop an inside job probably wouldn't be as easy. Now, is there anything else on your mind?"

"No, but aren't we here to learn what our job would consist of if we were to be employed?"

"Yes. I agree. But to inquire about an inside job... Vincent, you would have to be very close to someone who works for the company to even think of pulling off something so dishonest. Man, you don't sound like a student who's inquisitive about their job or what it consists of, and maybe you shouldn't be standing next to this bank vault nor its safe deposit box room. If I didn't know any better, I would think your comments were directed toward me."

"Just checking. You never know."

"Here! This is my business card with my private number. If you have any other security questions in line with our job, please feel free to give me a call."

I was throwing great hints to Ariana, and at no time did she ever give any indication of wanting to spend time with me, as Juncos had suggested. That to me was a bother and a red flag because getting the two of us to meet was Juncos's most pressing concern. Maybe it wasn't a paranoid moment I was having after all, because when Earl was away using the men's room, Ariana never cut our security discussion short. Could she have given my conversation more consideration than I thought and decided not to follow through on her brother's plan? She did show interest in what was an intriguing conversation, and she did give me her private number while watching Earl return from the men's room. She stated once he arrived that if we were still in school and needed further advice, to feel free to contact the bank through the school's counselor department. That came as a surprise after she had just given me her personal number.

As I mentioned earlier, Juncos's reason for being there in New York was obvious, and I wasn't letting him get to me. His sister was incredible, even in the way she handled my inquiries, but to gain my interest, I wasn't having it. I was too close to finishing school, and my intent was to let nothing get in the way of that, even if I were able to con her into a banking scheme.

Chapter 25. Tracking John Paul

"Vincent," Moke said, "you care for a coffee?" He stood in front of the snack counter at school. He was around a lot. If I didn't know any better, I'd think he was a student attending the private investigation school.

"No, but a chocolate milk would be fine. Are you buying?"

"You bet. Large or small?"

After we got our beverages, he dove right in. "Yo, dude, I know you love making extra money, scamming people with your card trick game on your lunch break, but today I think you should find time to look at what I have on your instructor's husband."

He was looking serious, and realizing in this moment how much he had grown over the years was surprising. "Okay. What do you suggest?"

"We could sit on the park bench and relax. Maybe lace a few joints and review the information I have on that real estate guy."

"A'right, Moke. Our break is over anyhow. I'll get back to class, and at lunch we'll meet at the same time, but not the usual spot. Meet me up by the north end of the park. Nobody likes sitting up there."

"Washington Square?"

"Yes. At the Fourth Street entrance."

"I'll be there."

***

He showed up on time, right as I was cleaning off the park bench.

"Smooth!" he called out, and that was a shock to me. Never in my presence had he ever called me by my nickname.

"Here!" he said, passing me a large brown paper bag that contained a legal-sized envelope with a voice-recording machine and a smaller white envelope filled with photos. He seemed very cautious, perhaps not wanting to upset me. "I'm sorry. I can't stay, but everything you need is in this bag."

He didn't give a specific reason for his departure, nor did I ask. I wanted to, but instead, I watched him walk toward the main street and out of sight.

After pulling out the contents, I threw the paper bag into the trash. The reason for the change in his demeanor became obvious as I sat on the bench and opened the legal-size envelope. What he obtained was simply too much to bear, way more than he was willing to sit and discuss knowing what was inside would be extremely infuriating and upsetting. John Paul and his assistant had been captured having extensive conversations. Inside the long white letter-sized envelope was a stack of photos. They were aligned in a series of occurrences, compiled, and completed for viewing. Though it took longer to receive the items from Moke than expected, overall, he did a thorough job, and what he had assembled could probably crush John Paul's reputation in the real estate business, where he was well known.

Those companions, whom he had led me to believe were his assistants, were much more than that. John was meeting his mistresses on most or all of his home showings. Then when I pushed play on the tape recorder, the sounds resonating from it were shocking.

It was unimaginable what it would do to his wife.

***

"Good evening, Ms. Lockhart. How're you today?" It was Monday evening, the thirtieth of May. I had entered our evening modeling class early as if everything were fine, knowing all along that what had been obtained would be devastating and damaging to the remainder of her life. There wasn't any other resolution but to share with her what I had discovered.

"I'm doing well, Mr. Lamond, and thanks for asking, but I must ask you—did something happen? Because John Paul is home in the evenings a lot more than usual. Vincent, could he have gained knowledge of our plan somehow? He's a very smart individual."

"No, Ms. Lockhart. It was too well planned. I don't suspect that would be the reason why."

"Well, do you have anything? Because this is killing me."

"What's killing you?"

"The fact that I'm not aware of what he's up to. He's home physically, but it's like his mind is someplace else."

There she goes calling me Vincent, again. Damn this dude. Well, it had to be said. There was no need to prolong her suffering.

"Ms. Lockhart, since I'm a few minutes early, could we meet in your audition room? We'd have a little more privacy there."

"Excellent. Give me about five minutes."

"No problem," I said.

Not long after entering the room, she began pacing a bit, as if she were overly anxious. "Please, Ms. Lockhart, why don't you have a seat? There's something you must know, and it's very alarming."

"Is it about him?"

"Yes! You must be warned though—it could have a detrimental effect on you."

"Vincent, there could be nothing more detrimental than living in fear of not knowing your husband. You must tell me. You must inform me of his actions."

"Okay, here. Take this. It's yours and remember—you can't say I didn't warn you."

"What is it?"

"It's the information you've been looking for."

"Thanks," she said to me. With that, I stood and watched, in a position to comfort her as she reached inside the larger envelope and pulled from it a smaller one that carried a stack of provocative and disgraceful photos. His behavior was too injurious for most to accept, and what was in that envelope was extremely baleful. After removing the pictures from the smaller envelope, she took a few minutes to scan through them. She then played a short version of the tape on the recorder, a fragment more than Ms. Lockhart was willing to withstand, so she shut it off.

"Vincent!" she yelled. "You have photographs of John Paul and another man, and they're both buck naked! What the hell is going on here? Shit, dude, after listening to that recorder, you mean my husband is gay, talking about leaving me, and for another man. And what the shit is with this whore? What is her part in this? Could she be this guy's wife?"

I felt sorry for the lady. She didn't deserve this. Nobody did. It wasn't likely the recorder was sitting close enough to capture a full conversation with the female, though it showed from the sequence of the photos that she walked into the condo much later, catching them together, causing anguish and leaving the lady upset and very aggrieved.

Looking at the photos wasn't helping Ms. Lockhart. Her face had begun to turn steaming red. Her anger mode had risen above a hundred Celsius. She seemed dreadfully bothered and horrified about facing her upcoming embarrassment.

"Ms. Lockhart, will you be all right?"

"Sure... It's a bit more than expected, but don't worry. I should be fine."

"I'm sorry that you had to experience this, Ms. Lockhart, but it looks to me that your husband was dating both of them. If you would take a look at the eighth photo in the smaller envelope... no way you could know this, but the female in that picture, she's the same person who accompanied him at our first home showing, the one I was led to believe was an assistant in training."

"This is a shame. What are you saying? The woman isn't this guy's wife?"

"No, Ms. Lockhart, I don't think she is. She, too, had stayed alone with John Paul after our first visit. I may not know what's normal after a showing, but the time they shared together was way past normal.

"Kourtney!" I said, using her first name as a show of compassion, "I'll leave you with this—your husband doesn't appear to be a good guy. And as for your cousin Mina, speaking on her behalf—that's why she left your home in the first place. Not because she was dating your husband, but because she realized what he was doing. She chose not to be around when the time came that you found out. Listen to me—you have enough material in those envelopes to make him dance to any tune you choose. Whatever you decide, whether it's staying with him or not, it's your decision."

"Stay with him? What the hell do you mean? I will pay to have his ass removed from this side of the Earth. Do you know of anyone who could do it for me?"

"No! That would be a very irrational decision. Give it some thought while you have the advantage. He has no idea yet that you're onto him. Besides, it will save you a great deal of discomfort, as you have so much to lose."

"To lose... what the heck do I have left? He has destroyed me. How will I be able to face my peers?"

"Why worry about them? They're not your friends. Ms. Lockhart, you're probably the only one who didn't know what your husband was doing. And that's okay, but don't throw all of what you've accomplished away with this unreasonable attitude of yours. Having him killed will only make things worse for you, something you would have to deal with from the inside of a prison cell. And if for some reason you were to get away with it, your conscience would suffer forever. He must pay, I agree, but think before you have this done because it's not a solution, it's a crime. And furthermore, the illegal things I've done for you thus far are already more than enough. My suggestion to you would be to contact an attorney. You have enough damaging information to disrupt his life forever, leaving him totally ruined."

"True, and you are probably right, but if I should come across someone who will, I'm going to have his ass murdered. He should not be able to do this to another person ever again."

"That's true, and I get it. He shouldn't be. However, count me out. I don't want any of this. I've done all I can." I shrugged my shoulders and held out my hands, palms up. "School will be over in a couple of months, and I would love to get out of here unharmed. But be that as it may, if your decision is to follow through with this, you'll not only ruin his life, but you'll destroy yours in the process."

"Thanks for all you've done, and don't worry, I'll be fine."

Nothing I was saying seemed to help in changing her mind. Ms. Lockhart was dead serious about having her husband killed. My services to her were no longer needed, especially after insisting there wasn't anything else illegal I was willing to do for her.

"Don't forget, Mr. Lamond—your final class photoshoot is this weekend. The photos are a very important part of your portfolio. Please be on time."

***

Later that night, a little before midnight, I walked into the apartment to find Karol still up. She was studying a financial statement from her job.

"Karol!" I called loudly enough to break her attention.

"Yes, Vincent? I'm trying to finish this work. What do you need?"

"Would you care to ride down to Macy's with me?"

"Macy's? When? What the heck do you want to buy from Macy's, and why?"

"Saturday! I'm having my final modeling photoshoot. I'll need a few new suits to pose in."

"Sure, I'll go with you, but I'm telling you right now—there's nothing you can buy at Macy's."

She didn't have a clue how much cash I had accumulated while there in New York, and I wasn't about to tell her. "That's okay. Somebody got-ta have a suit I can afford."

"Actually, I'm not so sure if I can, Vincent. I'm scheduled for a short workday on Saturday."

"Don't worry, we have plenty of time. Once you get here, we'll leave for Manhattan in the Monte Carlo. The photoshoot isn't until six o'clock."

***

Karol and I walked up and down the streets of Manhattan and found several suits for my photoshoot. Afterward, we headed to the school and even managed to arrive a bit early.

Exiting the Monte Carlo and walking toward the front entrance of the building, I found the door closed with a huge wreath hanging in the middle. I was stunned and confused, not knowing what to think or why a wreath would be on the front door. Normally, there was only one reason for such a wreath hanging on a locked door, and that was a death. With the wreath was a card, but it gave no identifying information.

Ms. Lockhart's death was the only thing running through my mind. *Man! What the hell have I gotten into? Shit! Could he have discovered what damaging information she had on him? Getting out-ta New York can't come fast enough.*

157

Fuck, things were getting scary, and on my way back to the car, I wondered for what reason that wreath was draped over the front door, and for whom.

"They're closed," I said with aggression while pulling the door handle of the Monte Carlo.

"Why, Vincent?"

"I'm not sure why."

"It's only five thirty. Was there a note?"

"Just a card—closed for personal reasons. But I'm positive the final photoshoot was today at six o'clock." I really didn't care to tell her about the wreath. I was wondering whether Ms. Lockhart was alive or if she really did go through with having her husband killed. It had only been a week since the excruciating news had been revealed to her about her husband.

No doubt that caused her to be a woman scorned, but was she really capable of murder? With my mind all bottled up, the sight of the wreath had begun to put fear into me. Still, I needed to remain calm. It would be devastating to Karol if she found out what was going on. I could sense her love for me was still there, and I cared dearly for her, as well, even though it had become clear to me there was no way we could ever live together. Karol was too good for me! Even so, there wasn't any need for her to know about Ms. Lockhart.

And speaking of her, my main objective was to find out if she was okay and if the wreath was meant for her.

"Vincent, I have an idea," Karol said, leaning her back against the passenger door, one leg across the other, her foot nearly touching the shifter of the Monte Carlo.

"What is it?" I asked.

"Why don't we have our own personal, private photoshoot?" she asked, sitting upright against the door happy and overly energetic. "We could design a background at the apartment and have it tonight."

Karol had no clue how much trouble I could be in. I was very alarmed by the wreath, mainly the reason for it, but she could not know this. I turned the ignition and started the Monte Carlo, turning to see if she could tell if something was bothering me. I smiled and turned up the stereo, and we listened to the Bee Gees sing "Staying Alive" while we cruised up Queens Boulevard back to the apartment.

Chapter 26. Searching for Protection

The next day while running around Brooklyn, I was confused and a little wary about what the hell was going on. I knew I needed to holler at Moke, but at that time it wasn't as important as the reason that had me traveling to 16th Street. Through the passenger-side window, there on the corner I saw Franco's bodega. Franco had told me to give him a call if ever I was in Brooklyn. I pulled over and stepped inside.

"Hi!" I kindly said to the clerk behind the register.

"Hello. May I help you?"

"Yes! I'm here for Francisco. Any way you can get word to him? My name is Vincent. Vincent Lamond."

"Sure. This must be your lucky day." The clerk must have touched a button because the phone rang. "Someone asking for you. Says his name is Vincent. Yes, sir. Lamond."

"My dude!" said Franco, who emerged from a back office. He spoke in what I'd call a true Brooklyn accent. "How long has it been? Three, four years maybe? How are you, Vincent?"

"I'm decent. What-ta 'bout yourself?"

"Well, as you can see, I'm still here. What brings you by?"

"Is there some place we can talk?"

"Sure. I'm headed to the warehouse. Would you like to come?"

"Yeah, why not?"

"Julia, hold down the store. We'll be right back."

We hopped in his truck, and he asked, "What brings you to Brooklyn?"

"Actually, it's more like what brings me to you. I may have gotten myself in a little trouble, and you said once if ever I was in Brooklyn to give you a holler. I wasn't sure about coming or if you could even help, but I figured it wouldn't hurt to ask."

"Yes, Vincent, I do recall. So how can I help? What's the depth of this trouble you're in?"

Maybe he couldn't do anything for me, but for the most part, his concern for my situation was positive. "Truthfully, Franco, I'm not sure. But there is an absolute uncertainty about one of my former coworkers, and there are serious discrepancies as to the reasons why he's in the city. Too many... In addition to that, another former coworker has brought to my attention that he isn't supposed to be here in the city at all. The fact is, he seems to be working for some agency, trying to gather and stockpile what they assume to be valuable and damaging information on me. On top of that, at one of the schools that I'm attending, a wreath is hanging from the door, causing me to have a strong belief that my instructor or her husband may have been murdered. Either way, Franco, I'll be in some type of trouble. It boils down to either being an accessory before the fact for gathering information on a cheating spouse and knowing my instructor may have conspired to have her unfaithful husband murdered. If not that, I'll being hunted down by her husband because of the information I gathered on him. Which may have led to *him* murdering *her.*"

"Wow, Vincent! I must say—you are in pretty damn deep."

"True! But I'm not waiting around just to see what happens."

"Smart move! But what can I do for you here in Brooklyn?"

"I need a weapon. All I got is this snub nose two-shot .38 derringer. Do you know of a place to score a nice piece that will let off at least seven rounds?"

He gave a smirky little smile. I had no hint what it was about. "Vincent, it appears that you're treading some deep waters. Hopefully, you'll be all right."

"I will, and don't give it another thought," I answered as he maneuvered his work truck through the rough streets of Flatbush. "My motto, Franco, has always been, 'Do unto others before others do unto you.' However, my first line of work is to find out who the damn wreath is for. When that has been determined, then I can adjust for my safety."

"Okay, Vincent, so as of now, you're not sure if either one of them is dead."

"No, I'm not, but I gave her a package that had all the lowdown on her cheating-ass husband."

"Well, it's either he's coming after you, or the cops will be looking for you. One thing for sure, my man—you're in some deep shit. And furthermore, there's only one reason for a posted wreath, and that's death."

"True! But I won't know who exactly it's for until classes resume on Monday."

He then looked over, pointed, and said, "This is it. We're here."

"Here where?" I asked.

"This is the warehouse."

We exited his truck to enter what I thought looked like a large manufacturing company.

"Shit, Frank! All of this is you?"

"Yes, the whole warehouse and everything in it. When you arrived, we needed some things for the store, and Julia had already planned this trip." He spoke with his head tilted to the right, a slight gleam to his eye. The guy looked prosperous as he viewed his spacious storeroom. There was merchandise all over the place, with tons of other items that couldn't even be sold in a store.

"Look around. Whatever you see that will fit your needs, you get it, and don't worry—it's all untraceable."

Damn! I couldn't believe what I was seeing.

"Oh, by the way—you mentioned a weapon that would let off at least seven rounds, right?"

"Yeah."

"Step in here. I call this my vault. Pick your poison, Vincent."

"Dammit, Franco, that .45 will work."

"Dude, that isn't a .45 you're looking at!"

"What the hell? It looks like one."

"Yes, it does. But that's a tranquilizer gun. It's used to subdue large animals. You'll love it. Let me show you how it works."

"That's fine, Franco, showing me how it works, but what good could it possibly do me?"

"Vincent, few can clamp their hands on one of these. Listen, if there's ever anything you need done, and your intent is not to kill, this is what you would want. Take it. It's yours, and here's several syringes. And take this as well—it's a Beretta 92. It hasn't hit the market yet, and you'll be one of the first in the US to have one. Don't worry, my man! It's strapped with a full 10-round clip. Keep them both. Be careful, though, and watch yourself."

"Sure! But how much?"

"No charge. Anyone with enough guts to drive down Flatbush Avenue alone and park on some of the most tenacious streets in Brooklyn is all right with me."

I gave him a firm handshake and a man hug, just to show my gratitude and appreciation.

***

Back at the store, Franco turned to me as I opened the door. "Vincent, remember—I'm in the outreach business. It's always better to listen than to speak, which you did. Be careful."

"Don't worry, I will!" I hopped out of his truck and looked back through the passenger-side window, confused, and not realizing exactly what his statement actually meant.

"In that case, scream back when you know it's safe."

"You got it. Stay low."

***

I hadn't spoken with Moke for a minute, not since he had dropped off the bag. I still owed him for that. Then my mind clicked. If I were traveling up Kings Highway, I could just run over to Moke's granny's house, where he was living.

"Come in," Moke's grandmother said.

"How are you, Mama Moses? I haven't seen you in a few weeks. Here, I know how you love pizza, so I stopped to get you one. I hope you enjoy it." It may not have been normal to stop and do this for her, but shit—there wasn't anything normal about me.

"I'm quite sure I will."

Moke's granny was that one person you'd need while spending time in Brownsville. Brooklyn was slightly dangerous, but she had been living on the same street in Brownsville for over forty years and had the respect of everyone in her neighborhood. She claimed to have seen more dead people than I had fingers, but everybody gave Mama Moses a pass, including some of the most dangerous street hustlers in the hood.

"Thank you, Vincent. There should be more young men like you in the world. It doesn't hurt to be respectful and to show a little decency. Moke is upstairs. Says he hasn't seen you for a while. I think he's been looking for you. Wait here. I'll be right down."

Soon afterward, they both appeared in the living room. Mama Moses picked up the pizza and headed toward the kitchen. "Vincent, thanks again. You boys be careful 'cause it's a lot going on around here."

"What's good, Moke? Your granny said you been looking for me?"

"Yeah, Vincent. Our neighbor a couple of doors down was killed this week. Man, I got-ta get out of here. This is not for me."

If I could only make it through the next month, his problem would be solved, I thought. "Okay, Moke. Here's your package for the photos and the tape. It's six hundred bucks. Hopefully, it'll make you feel better. Hey, by the way, graduation is next month. If you're really ready, you could leave with me." I was trying my best to lift his spirits, even though I had no idea how I would fare with that.

"No, man! You have your son to care for. You can't just up and leave."

Moke was right about DeVaan, but I had begun to put them at risk, and that couldn't continue. People were coming at me from all angles, and things had gotten serious. I had to make a move, maybe sooner than expected.

***

The next morning was Monday, the sixth of June, and we were on our first break. I'd just sat down at my favorite table to enjoy a chocolate milk and honey bun when a guy who called himself Korey pulled up a chair and sat across from me.

"Hey, man," he said, hat turned backward.

"Yeah, what's good, my dude?"

"Do you have any of those laces for sale?"

I couldn't help but stare at him, and afterward I focused my attention solely on our surroundings. Mind you, we were almost ready to graduate, and everyone in class knew how it was done. We'd been there for nearly a full school term, and nobody had ever asked me to sell them anything directly.

"Korey, right?"

"Yeah."

"Who sent you to me?"

"No one."

"Have you ever seen me with a lace stick before?"

"No, but they said you were the man."

"Who are they, and again, who sent you?"

"Nobody! Just the word on the block. Everyone from the park said you had them."

Obviously, he was lying, and someone had sent him because Moke was the only one who had passed loose toothpicks in the park. I never believed in any illegal tradeoff for cash. It wasn't my style. Always too risky. The scenario playing out here was one of the oldest and most commonly used cop tricks in the game.

"Look, Korey, since you're being loyal to your source, what if I double what they're paying you? I won't even ask for a name. Just nod your head if he has a class with me."

I was covering myself in case he was wired. That way, no one would know his answer. *Juncos could be behind his approach to my table*, I thought. He knew I would be sitting on the preordered joints, and if he could get me to sell just one to someone I thought was a classmate, he would have me. He never gave a nod one way or the other, and that left me suspicious, so I cut our conversation short.

Juan seemed to be aware of my every move, though he couldn't quite keep up. During one of my earlier conversations with my friend Newt from the previous job, I learned Juan had not been performing his duties at the investigative school. Word was he would soon be returning to his regular job, leading me to believe time was running out for him to get me into an interrogation room. Juncos was getting desperate. That meant he had to come up with something soon. If not, the agency he was working for would soon pull him from the case. Newt still wasn't sure of what agency had sent him, but he did know that Juan Juncos wasn't in a logistics class for the company.

Chapter 27. Checking on Ms. Lockhart

"Mrs. Tyler, do you have a minute?" I asked as she walked past me at the water fountain in the hallway of the modeling school. I was still unsettled about the wreath, and it seemed impossible to get enough water to clear my throat. Mrs. Tyler was the school's top administrator. She and Ms. Lockhart were very close, and she was the one person who would have genuine insight into who exactly the wreath was meant for.

"Yes, Vincentius!" I was surprised that she called me by my full first name. "How can I help you? By the way, your name is incredibly unique. Have you ever researched the meaning?"

"Not recently, but a time or two I have."

"Powerful meaning it has, Mr. Lamond."

"Thanks, Mrs. Tyler. Apart from that, we were supposed to have our final photoshoot on Saturday evening, but when I arrived, there was no one here. There was only a wreath draped over the front door. If I may ask, who was it for?"

"Oh! You didn't know?"

"No! Know what?" She made it seem as if something had happened to Ms. Lockhart.

"Come with me. I'll explain it to you, but first, there's a call I have to take care of. Please, have a seat. This will only take a minute."

As I sat on a little love seat with my back against the wall facing Mrs. Tyler's office, the secretary asked, "Could I get you a magazine or something?"

"No, I'm okay." I had no idea who she called. She was talking with her door closed. The truth was—that call only took several minutes, but it seemed like a lifetime. Through the frosted glass I saw she had finished the call and was now removing herself from behind her desk.

"Where were we?" she asked after reappearing.

"You were beginning to discuss the reason for the wreath."

"Oh, yes! I'm sorry, Mr. Lamond. Please, come in. With everything that's going on, I lost my train of thought. Ms. Lockhart wanted me to call her as soon as you arrived this evening. She wanted me to give you this envelope as well. She will not be with us for a while. She's out indefinitely."

That means she's alive, but where in the hell is John Paul?

"Vincentius... can I call you that?"

"Lamond, if you don't mind. It has always been the school's policy to address people by last names."

"Absolutely. That's fine with me. Mr. Lamond it is. Anyway, last Tuesday morning Ms. Lockhart and her husband got into a heated discussion. She made the mistake of picking a quarrel with him. Something about a picture she found and left lying on top of their television set."

"What type of picture, Mrs. Tyler?"

"Regrettably, Ms. Lockhart received a photo, somehow, of John Paul and another guy. She did not go into extensive details, but she did mention to me, Mr. Lamond, that you would be aware of the photo. I didn't ask her how that came about, and she didn't give any particulars. She just gave me the envelope to give to you. Though she did state that the picture was awfully embarrassing."

Mrs. Tyler told me that on Friday, John Paul's girlfriend showed up there at the school. She had information to solidify the truth about John Paul and his boyfriend being together, proclaiming she was present when the picture in question was taken.

Man, I could only shake my head and ask, "What happened while the girlfriend was at the school? Did someone get killed? Was that the purpose of the wreath?"

"No, Mr. Lamond, no! The wreath you saw... that was in honor of the building owner. He passed away Friday, the same day John's girlfriend was here."

I breathed a sigh of relief. At least nobody I knew had died.

"Mr. Lamond, the girlfriend was so overcome and heartbroken that she went to Ms. Lockhart earlier in the week. She told her all about their relationship and the affair she had with her husband. Most importantly, the girlfriend stated that she didn't know about the boyfriend until the day of the picture in question."

"What actually happened to Ms. Lockhart? Is she all right?"

"Yes, Vincent! I'm sorry. Mr. Lamond. My mistake. She should be okay. From my understanding, the bickering and arguing continued well into late Wednesday, until John Paul snapped. Early that Thursday morning, when Ms. Lockhart finally awakened, she found herself lying in the hospital. I'm sorry to say, Mr. Lamond, but she has several cracked ribs, a badly bruised face, and a broken right arm.

"Vincent! I didn't realize you and Kourtney had developed such a personal relationship that you were on a first-name basis." Mrs. Tyler had called me Vincent again, but this time it didn't seem to be by mistake. It appeared to me she was searching for information.

"Mrs. Tyler, I wasn't aware of that. May I ask, what gives you that assumption?"

"During our general and sometimes social conversations, oftentimes I would find Ms. Lockhart addressing you as Vincent."

"Since they were general conversations, couldn't it have been easier for her to use that instead of Mr. Lamond?"

"Huh! Easier to use Vincent..." she said sarcastically, as if she didn't believe Ms. Lockhart wasn't calling me Vincent.

"Mrs. Tyler, how far back can you remember Ms. Lockhart ever calling me Vincent in your presence? Because at no time at school in the past, on no occasion during the term, has she ever done so. She is undeniably a great instructor, a professional inside and out of her classroom. Not ever during school has there been a personal relationship between the two of us, and under no circumstances were we ever on a first-name basis. I've never been in the practice of calling her Kourtney."

Explaining this to Mrs. Tyler and trying to ascertain her thoughts on our relationship was becoming very unpleasant. "Exactly what are you insinuating? Surely, you don't think a relationship between the two of us could have caused their argument?"

"Well, Mr. Lamond, you two have been seen together a lot at the end of the school term. Generally, that would draw attention and cause assumptions to be made, wouldn't you think?"

"Assumptions! Huh!" I giggled a little. "Everybody makes them, Mrs. Tyler. Is there anything else?"

"No, Mr. Lamond, that's it. Hey, wait—there is one thing. I never got the meaning of your first name. Do you know?"

"Yes." I wanted so badly to trade the meaning of my name for how much she really knew about Ms. Lockhart's scheme. Actually, there wasn't any sure way of knowing how much information Ms. Lockhart was sharing, so I decided to hold off.

"Vincentius is a conqueror. One who wins. Winning over evil, I'm told."

"Interesting! Very enlightening, Mr. Lamond."

"I have to run, Mrs. Tyler," I said after grabbing the envelope and stuffing it into my back pocket.

"Since there wasn't a photoshoot Saturday, and no classes today, will class resume tomorrow?"

"No, Mr. Lamond. There won't be any classes for the rest of the week. We do apologize for that."

I turned and left the building. After making it to the Monte Carlo, I placed the white envelope above the dashboard on top of the Bible. I sat for several minutes pondering everything Mrs. Tyler had just discussed with me. As heartless as I was, what happened to Ms.

Lockhart truly bothered me. She really didn't deserve what he had done. I reached again for the envelope and read—

Mr. Lamond, I would like to admit as I lie in this hospital bed, I am deeply confused. I hardly know you, but it's like you're the only person I can truly trust to confide in. Not only am I hurting from bruises and broken bones, but I'm also pregnant. Now you are the only person other than the hospital personnel who knows.

I've been seriously contemplating aborting this child because John Paul is not deserving of one. Only, that would be totally against my religion and everything that I've been morally taught. If I were to end my pregnancy, it would mean that I would be murdering my child. And, whatever the gender, he, or she, they would not deserve that. Once you told me to think first because I had way too much to lose... well, you were right, even though I didn't realize it at the time, and for that, I thank you.

Vincent, John was arrested Thursday afternoon, and I think he'll be released tomorrow on Friday, and I'm told he'll probably have some people come after you. During a break between one of our massive fallouts when we were back and forth at each other's throats, he rustled through my personal records and found your student profile information. He became enraged and promised to visit you at your apartment. But before any of that comes to fruition, I would love to see you once more before you leave. Here is the hospital information, and I also have a settlement package of four grand for all the work you've done. One other thing before I close this letter—will you please find Mina and bring her to the hospital?

"Wow!" I drew a deep gust of air and blew it back into the atmosphere with exertion, thanking God she wasn't dead.

***

Finding Mina wasn't a problem. She didn't do very much. Her life was simple, and I was certain she would love to see her cousin again.

After visiting Mina and enlightening her on what had happened to Ms. Lockhart, she was eager to come. I promised to pick her up early Thursday morning, the ninth of June.

School had already been canceled for the week, and the week was moving fast. That Thursday, honoring what Ms. Lockhart had asked of me, I fetched the Monte Carlo and was soon on the road fighting traffic. The Long Island Expressway was the most efficient way of getting to Mina's place. Once I arrived, she hopped in, then we fought the same traffic back to the hospital. The main entrance to the parking garage was right off the boulevard. We pulled up to its automatic barricade and waited for the extended arm to rise. If the wards of the hospital were anything like the parking garages, then they were busy.

Ms. Lockhart's room was on the third level. As the elevator was lifting us to her floor, my thought was to get this visit over with as soon as possible. After making it to her room, I stood just outside watching Mina embrace her cousin, who had begun to cry. She even had me teary-eyed as I continued to watch. *Shit!* I said to myself because it was shocking to see her in that position, tubes going everywhere, one arm in a sling hanging from a support bracket... it looked horrible.

Unfortunately, Ms. Lockhart didn't look or seem to be feeling very well. She had been badly beaten—to the point she could hardly move her body. Her ribs were in terrible shape, and her eyes would squint every time she moved. My anger boiled, and if John Paul was coming after me, my only thought was to move first, as he was still locked up.

This was no different from any other message or warning that someone was coming to kick your ass. Information like this shouldn't be taken lightly and definitely not ignored. I wanted to follow his ass from the first step he took after being released from the county jail. I knew I didn't have time for that, but someone who did crossed my mind. Big E from the strip club, he could do it. If he knew danger was upon me, he'd have John Paul and his associates taken care of before anything happened.

Of course, I had obtained a larger weapon that could take his ass out, more than likely with one round. But bug that shit! All I wanted was to get the hell out of New York City and never once have to worry about John Paul again.

"I'm done, Vincent," Mina said. "She's waiting to see you. I'll be in the waiting room down at the end of the hall."

"Okay. Once I'm finished, I'll be right there." I quietly stepped inside. Ms. Lockhart was hurting badly and could hardly move. Still, she reached under her covers and somehow made it to her chest with an envelope.

"Take this," she whispered. "It's for you. Thank you."

I couldn't see prolonging my stay. Nearly in tears myself, I gave her a light hug and departed the room. Mina and I left the hospital and barely spoke a word going back to her place.

Not long after dropping her off, I returned to the apartment. Karol met me at the door with some information about a very important phone call.

"Vincent, do you know a Sergeant Moke?"

"Yes, why?" I didn't have time for anything other than John Paul at the present time, but I had to at least stop and listen to what she had to say.

"He'd like for you to call him. Says it's important, and he suggests you call right away."

"Okay, but right now I can't. I have to drive to South Jersey, so he'll have to wait." Making sure she and my son would be safe was much more important than whatever was going on in South Carolina with Sergeant Moke.

"All right, Vincent, but this guy sounded serious."

"Don't worry, I'll work it out." With everything going on around me, it had become a must that I reach out to Big E. Rather than calling Moke's dad, I called Moke instead. I needed him to ride with me.

Even if John Paul didn't appear to be the violent type, you tend to pay attention when someone sends you a warning signal, especially after what he did to Ms. Lockhart. I needed to protect myself... Although John Paul was a low-down, no-good, disrespectful, abusive, cheating-ass husband who needed to be checked, he didn't deserve to be killed.

Chapter 28. Big E's Deal

Stopping in Brooklyn and grabbing Moke to ride I-95 with me to Big E's place was like securing a bodyguard. He could help deter what was likely to happen if I were to travel alone. Besides, he needed to know how serious things had gotten. Along with that, having another set of eyes to look out for me wouldn't hurt. One thing about Moke—he wasn't that shy individual we once knew. He had changed and really grown into a different person.

I knew Mama Moses would be gone when I got there, so I parked, ran inside for a quick piss, washed my hands, and we left for Cherry Hill.

While we traveled the turnpike, I felt it was best to let Moke in on why I needed him to ride with me. However, before I could speak, he asked, "Vincent, who is this guy you're going to see, and why are you in such a rush?"

"Rush? I'm not rushing, but I do need to make a quick move before John Paul does."

"What's the deal with him?"

"He whipped the living crap out of his wife, then told her that he'd be sending someone after me for giving that information to her."

"How could he tell it was you, Vincent? Who gave it to her? I could barely tell who you were under that disguise."

"That's part of the reason we're going to see this guy—because John Paul whipped her until she told. He shouldn't have touched Ms. Lockhart. Moke, I don't have the time to deal with him, and if I did, it would be taking too big of a risk to do something to him without an alibi."

Pulling into the city via Kings Highway brought back memories, and those memories came with an understanding. Even with Moke's continuous growth into a different person, I couldn't take a chance on carrying him out to Big E's compound. Big E didn't care for you bringing others to his office that he didn't know. More went on at Earnest's place than strippers and dancers holding on to a pole, so a new face without an invite was inappropriate. My plan was to drop Moke off at one of my favorite places, Big Mama's Diner.

"Moke, I prefer a spot where my back can be against the wall," I said as we looked for a table. It was midday, close to 1:30 p.m., so Moke had time for a delicious meal as he waited, one served with a side of some of the best hot water cornbread ever made in America and finished with a piece of cake so good, it would be hard not to eat all of it.

"Order me a large strawberry Kool-Aid when you place your order. I'll be right back. I need to make this call."

From a pay phone outside Big Mama's, I gave Big E a ring.

"Earnest speaking. What can I do for you?"

"Big E! It's Vincent. Do you have a minute?"

"A minute!" he answered surprisingly loud. "Where are you?"

"You'd probably not believe it, but I'm in town."

"Cool. Just tell me where. I'll come to you."

"I'm at the corner of Second and—"

"Say no more. You're at Big Mama's restaurant."

"Yeah."

"Hey, dude, you still strutting those sport jackets?"

"Yeah, you know it."

"Okay, hold tight. I'll be right there."

Stepping back inside, I was impressed watching Moke blend in with everyone, including the regular lunch patrons. I remember a time when this dude wouldn't even take a lunch break.

A little less than twenty minutes later, a fellow dressed all in black walked in, scanned the restaurant for a second, then came straight to our table. I looked over at Moke, then focused my attention back on the guy.

"Are you Vincent?"

"Why you ask?"

"I'm from the club. The jacket. He said you'd be wearing one."

"Who said?"

"Big E."

"Yes, I'm Vincent! Then you must be riding with Earnest."

"Damn! You guys must be close," the huge gentleman said, giving me one hell of a look.

"Why is that?"

"Three months with Big E... I've never heard him called Earnest."

"Huh! Maybe you should keep it that way." I took a sip of the strawberry Kool-Aid and stood up. "Wait here, Moke. Lead the way, sir. By the way, I didn't get your name."

"Fortune! Everybody calls me Big Fortune."

"I can see why."

"Let's roll," he said with a gentle smile. Once we stepped out of Big Mama's diner, I beheld a black-on-black stretch limo with four-inch gangster whitewalls, parked alongside the fence. The car took up several parking spots, like Big E owned the damn place. Once I was close enough, he let down his window and beckoned with his index finger.

"Vincent, get in."

After climbing into what looked to be a miniature living room, I went on to inform him of what my needs were and how badly I wanted to get my diplomas. Not to leave anything out, I decided to admit what I had done in digging up information on John Paul and how it led to the hospitalization of his wife. I also explained he could have others coming after me once he was released.

Big E was dangerous, but he was also a family man who valued women above all else. He believed they were God's most precious creation, and anyone who abused a female was trash.

"Vincent, what would you like to happen to this person?" he asked, sitting back in his spacious and beautiful machine. "There're several ways we can handle this, but it's all up to you." Big E had taken care of situations for me previously in the past.

"Not as aggressively as with Mike, Big E, but enough hurt that will stick to his forehead as a reminder."

He leaned forward and looked directly into my eyes. "You mean not to waste him?"

"Right. He's having a kid. He doesn't know it, but his wife is pregnant. So no, don't waste'm. I just want him off my back."

"Wise decision! We can manage that for you. Here's the deal—I have a package that needs to be dropped at a senator's house in Bridgeport, Connecticut. Can you make that happen?"

Brushing the sides of my mustache with my thumb and index finger, I said, "Connecticut, huh?"

He didn't answer, only kept his gaze fixed on me.

"The package is my only tradeoff for getting this guy off my back?"

"Yes. Just make the drop."

I didn't foresee a problem with that. Big E was one of the few I believed in (even though I trusted no one). Never once did I think he would put me in harm's way.

"In Bridgeport, you say?"

"Yeah, and don't worry—you'll be covered on both ends. Consider the job done. I have two of the best. They'll paper bag and pumpkin swell his head until every damn time the thought of you arises, his fricking head will start hurting. Vincent, when those guys show up, they'll have the package with all the necessary instructions. You follow those exactly to the Bridgeport drop, and you'll be fine."

It seemed to be a much better option than putting a stop to John Paul myself and possibly ending up in prison. "Okay, E. We have a deal."

Afterward, we sat and discussed the details of where I would meet his guys and where exactly John Paul could be found. I explained he was scheduled to be released from the county jail soon, but that could not be confirmed yet. I also placed emphasis on the fact that the borough of Queens was only a little over two hours away, and the package exchange could take place there. The Queens Hotel on the Boulevard would be perfect for us to meet. I would receive the package with instructions, and they could learn exactly where John Paul would be residing.

Big E seemed satisfied with the plan and praised me for wanting to protect Ms. Lockhart and her child. "Great, Vincent. Like I told you once before—go do you."

***

"Hey, man, is everything all right?" Moke asked when I rejoined him inside Big Mama's. He was licking the juices from some of the best pigs' feet on the planet from his fingertips. "Will you be able to get this dude off your back?" He seemed more afraid of what John Paul would do to me than I was.

"Sure, Moke, provided all goes well. Don't worry so much. You'll give yourself a damn heart attack. Come on, let's go."

There were other issues that needed to be addressed, like his father's phone call that Karol had mentioned earlier. It was a bit surprising to hear from him and difficult to figure out the purpose of his call. What the heck could he want with me? Maybe Mama Moses knew. There were two killings on her block, and maybe she knew more than what she could tell. But what would that have to do with him calling me? He must have felt his son was involved in something. And whatever that something was, it must've been getting too close to his family.

But here I was again, assuming what others were thinking. Heck, Mama Moses had been on that damn block way before I was even born. That he wouldn't be worried about. It had to be something else. My mind continued to search but with no results.

179

After hitting the turnpike, I turned my attention back to Moke. "Hey dude, when was the last time you talked to your dad? He called me earlier, but I wasn't home. You have any idea what that call could be about?"

"No!"

"Do you guys keep in touch?"

"We don't communicate much, but Bee-Bee called a few times. She tells me he's still angry because I left and never joined the church. Vincent, I've never mentioned it, but she said to tell you hi, and she's still looking forward to seeing you again. Oh, I almost forgot, she also told me to tell you she made this semester's honor roll."

"Dang, man, you are not that old. How in the heck you forget so much?"

"I don't forget. You never sit still long enough for anyone to tell you anything."

"Did she mention anything about Lilah?"

"No. She hardly speaks of her anymore since you left town. I don't understand what could've happened between them. They've been friends since grade school. Vincent, was it anything you did?"

"Why you ask me that?"

"Man, it wasn't like that before we showed up, and once you left, *everybody* seemed different."

"Ion know, Moke. If it was, I'm sorry."

If his sister wasn't telling him anything about their relationship, I wasn't going to overstep my boundaries and inform him. I thought once I got back to Queens, I'd call his dad to find out what he wanted. It had begun to bother me, but first I had to find out the status of John Paul. Staying a step ahead of him was important, especially if I were to live by my own proverb, "Do unto others before others do unto you."

Moke had gotten quiet over on his side of the Monte Carlo since our conversation about his sister, but the closer we got to Sutter

Avenue in Brownsville, the more Moke's leg shook as if it were about to depart from his fricking kneecap. Not for one moment was I ever aware before dropping him off that Brownsville had become a dangerous place for him.

It wasn't very late, so I turned off the car and went inside. "Hey, Mama Moses, just coming to speak to you before heading home," I said.

"I'm glad you did, Vincent. Come into the kitchen for a minute. I need to ask you something."

"Yes ma'am..." After sitting at the table, she asked, "Vincent is it anything you can tell me about some pills Moke is supposed to be selling in the neighborhood? I've heard there nearly killing people if you know you should say something."

"No! Mama Moses, I don't have a clue."

"Alright, then you be careful out there, Vincent."

"Don't worry, I will." Maybe that's the reason he was so quiet.

I left and went directly over to Mina's apartment in Long Island, hoping she and her cousin were still enthusiastic about being reunited. I buzzed her apartment, not knowing what the outcome would be but thinking Mina had to be my best shot at finding out anything about John Paul.

"Who's there?"

"It's Vincent."

"Hold up, I'll be right down." Her voice seemed magical coming through the intercom and had the makings of a welcome greeting. After making it downstairs, Mina stepped outside with the greatest smile on her face.

"What's going on, Vincent?"

"Any updates on Ms. Lockhart and John Paul since this morning?"

"Not really. The nurse claims she's recovering well and healing wonderfully. The little one, my baby cousin, is doing good as well."

"That's really great, considering the damage John Paul could have caused."

"True, Vincent. I agree." We looked each other in the eye and fell into a serious hug and loving embrace.

"Okay, then," I said, forgetting half the reason I was there. "Take care of yourself."

"Wait... We did find out that John Paul hasn't been released. Tomorrow is Friday. The earliest would be Monday."

"Seriously? Why Monday? What happened? Did you find out?"

"Yes! Since Kourtney was pregnant at the time she was severely beaten, the state is filing additional charges and will be asking for a bond increase. All of that will delay John's release till at least Monday. And one other thing, Vincent—she claims he'll be coming for you once he's released."

"No shit! Well, shut da front door."

"Okay."

"Not you, it's just an expression, but I do have to get going. Help take care of her, Mina, and thanks for the information."

***

The meeting took place the next Friday, the seventeenth of June, at the Queens Hotel. With the power of Mina's information, everyone at the meeting could sit back and relax with smiles on their faces, leaving me free from that extra hustle of finding him and with more time to prep for the Bridgeport drop. I explained to them the scenario for John Paul's release, and they told me to relax. Everything would be fine, and I would never have to worry ever about John Paul again.

In return, I was given a medium-sized box with a note taped to the bottom. I was told to keep the contents frozen until I was ready to leave for the drop, and everything needed, including all instructions, was attached to the bottom.

With the meeting ending, we all departed. I still didn't know exactly what I would be carrying to Bridgeport, but knowing I had no place to freeze the box, I had to hurry up to the Bronx to Will's place. He was the only person I had enough faith to risk this box with, and not only that—he also had a freezer in his basement, one that could be used until I was ready to leave for Bridgeport.

After getting in touch with Will and explaining exactly what I needed, everything after that began to fall into place. I even reached out to Big E for the last time before making the trip, with him informing me that the Senator would be alone at his home if everything worked as scheduled and the instructions on the bottom of the box were followed precisely.

On Monday evening, the twentieth of June, I picked up the package from Will's and headed up to Connecticut, knowing I needed to be there by dark, per the instructions from the box. The instructions were very detailed and gave explicit information on how to approach and open the senator's gate.

Damn! I thought as the large black iron gate began to slide to my right. While waiting to enter, I shook my head at the size of his house. After pulling in, I began to get a little jittery, not knowing what I was about to encounter with the damn box. The note instructed me to follow the driveway all the way to the large birdbath in the middle of the circular drive, continue around the circle, and pull into the smaller drive just to the east of the bath.

The note also stated: *It may look as though you can't park there, but you can. It's a private drive that only the senator and his close associates use. The door chime will automatically ring when you pull in.*

And just like that, someone was standing in front of a set of extremely large, unnatural-sized doors. I was to carry the box to the front, deliver it only to the senator, and open the box as the senator watched. That had me nervous as hell, but it was either that or deal with the possibility of having to take care of John Paul myself. I considered the act to be the lesser of two evils. The instructions stated: *While standing at the door, use the pre-attached razor from the bottom of the box to cut it open. Once the box is completely open, hand it to the senator.*

"Here, sir!" I said, helping to unwrap the plastic. I took a quick peek inside, and chills flowed throughout my body. There was half of someone's arm inside, with the ring finger detached and sitting in the bottom of the box. It was placed to one side, a huge, solid diamond ring still wrapped around it. The senator gave me a small envelope, said thanks, turned completely around with the box, and closed the door.

Remember now, I was only twenty-five and raised in a small town. I wasn't a New York City-type gangster, so witnessing something so violent may have been a bit much to stomach. I wasn't the praying type either, but if I were, I'd pray not for me but for the guy who lost his arm. I had no idea whether he was a current or former US senator. I just followed the instructions. Never at any time did I inquire about the package, and no—I never found out whose arm it was.

My only thought after delivering the box was to find my way out and back to I-95 southbound as quickly as possible. *Calm yourself,* I thought while experiencing a flashback from a few years ago when I got four speeding tickets all in one day. After remembering that and acknowledging the excessive speed I was traveling at, I calmed. Then it crossed my mind to open the small but thick envelope, which I assumed was packed with a profuse amount of detailed follow-up instructions.

I pulled into a Sunoco service station to get gas and opened the envelope. Surprisingly, it had fifty crisp one-hundred-dollar bills banded together. Five grand with no further instructions. Neither Earnest nor his guys explained anything about a return package, and

Big E had already told me everything would be covered on both ends. "Go do you," was all that was said to me.

My decision was to keep it. I slipped Willie Hutch's "Brother's Gonna Work it Out" into the cassette player and continued south.

Chapter 29. Clearing a Path for Departure

"Vincent," my instructor called, "could you come to the front, please?"

It was Thursday morning on the twenty-third of June, and we were all sitting around in different areas of the classroom discussing our post-graduation plans. After running around South Jersey and Bridgeport, I was tired and had been a little late. After already missing several days of school, my instructor advised me to report to the administrator's office, so I headed down the hall to her office.

"Good morning, Vincent!"

"Ms. Whitley, how are you?"

"I'm doing well. Vincent, do you know an Officer Staten? Says he's from Oklahoma."

"Yes! What-ta bout him?" I had not seen or heard from Officer Staten since he and Agent Rhea Collins were together in Ferriday, Louisiana, last year. "He was here at the school needing to speak with you."

"Ms. Whitley, he's a city detective. Why would he be here in New York? Did he give you a reason why he needed to see me?"

"No, but he did leave his card and told me that he would be back tomorrow morning."

I didn't care to speak to any type of officer. All I wanted was to leave New York City. "Ms. Whitley, since I've already completed all my finals, would it be okay if you were to mail my diploma to my hometown address in Ferriday, Louisiana?"

"I don't see a problem with that. You're only waiting on the actual graduation date to formally receive your diploma. But if you don't mind me asking—are you in some kind of trouble?"

"Not that I know of, but could you tell me if you happened to see Juan Juncos in the company of this officer?"

"No, I didn't see the two of them together, though Juan did show up immediately after Officer Staten's departure. Didn't think anything of it. Why would Juan be of interest to this Officer Staten?"

"I'm not one hundred percent sure, but it's a strong possibility the two of them may be working together. Juan is not a regular student. I'm positive about that. One of my former coworkers has already confirmed that he shouldn't be here in New York."

"Vincent, that sounds a little farfetched."

"It does, Ms. Whitley, but I believe it to be the truth."

"Juan and I previously worked for the same state ID card and vital statistics processing center. Occasionally, different forms and blank IDs would come up missing from their sequence. I've been told that the ID blanks and other valuable forms that were missing from various departments had been discovered in a series of crimes. Being head of that department, I was placed under high-profile surveillance. For the most part, nothing has ever come of it, but several former employees would always tell me to be careful because I was being watched."

"What proof is there to validate your suspicion of him?"

"I've been told from a reliable source that Juan was scheduled for a logistics and distribution class in St. Louis, a coverup for his stay here in New York. I've also been informed that he has to return to his previous job in the near future if he hasn't found a way to at least get me into an interrogation room. There's too much proof that he isn't supposed to be here to address. Please, you have to take this seriously. And how I know all of this is the biggest reason I chose this school—to learn how to think and act like a cop."

"Are you sure you're not in any trouble?"

"Like I mentioned earlier, no. I'm not in any type of trouble that I know of, but could you do me a favor?"

"I'm not sure. Maybe. As long as it doesn't affect our administration. What else can I help you with, aside from mailing your diploma?"

"Once Officer Staten returns, could you not tell him I asked about Juncos?"

"Why is that?"

"Because I'm almost positive they don't realize I'm aware of Juncos following me."

"Sure! No one has to know the extent of our conversation. Is there a number where you can be reached?"

I hated to tell her, but the truth was I had no forwarding number.

***

It had come time to finalize everything at both schools. However, I had not yet explained to Mrs. Tyler at the modeling school that I would be leaving the next weekend and needed that diploma mailed to me as well. When I walked into her office that evening, I could tell something was wrong. She hurried to close the door behind me, and the way she looked was frightening.

"What's wrong, Mrs. Tyler? Why are you so nervous?"

"Vincent, have a seat."

"I'm good. I prefer to stand if you don't mind."

"That's good. It may be best that you do."

"What is it, Mrs. Tyler?"

"Vincent, have you heard from Kourtney?"

"No, I haven't. Not lately. Why are you asking? Is she all right? I'm only here to inform you that I'll be departing next weekend and to tell you where my diploma should be mailed."

"I see."

"Is she all right?" I asked again a few decibels higher. "And what is going on with everyone being called by their first name?"

"Yes, to answer your question, she's getting much better. Though the same can't be said for you."

"What-ta you mean? I'm fine, Mrs. Tyler."

"Are you?"

"Yes, I am! What the heck are you getting at?"

"Vincent! Did you do anything to John Paul?"

"No, I didn't. What happened to him?"

"Man, it's serious. John has been maimed and left with near-fatal injuries."

She started to fill me in on how the cops were looking to question me about the beating of John Paul nearly to death. This was the first I had heard of him being injured.

"Vincent... Mr. Lamond... whatever you prefer to be called—a few days ago, John was found at one of his home showings, alone and beaten to the point he's almost unrecognizable. His face and head have swollen so much, the paper bag that was placed over it had bulged to the point of splitting. His nose was broken to where he could barely breathe. They say he can hardly see from something called a pumpkin head beating. His eyes are nearly swollen shut. I'm also told that the cops are looking for you and your friend concerning John's injuries. Vincent, if you don't mind telling me, what is a pumpkin head beating?"

"Mrs. Tyler, I don't know, so I can't tell you, though it seems obvious what it is. And, furthermore, I don't know when this was supposed to have happened or how you acquired this information. For the most part, I've been out of town for several days. Whatever happened to him, it wasn't me or my friend who did it. Regardless to what you think, Mrs. Tyler I have to go, but you can send my diploma to this address, and for the last time, I didn't do anything to Ms. Lockhart's husband.

Damn, I have to get inside that apartment while Karol is at work to pack my stuff. If I'm to keep them safe, I need to get away. I refuse

***

"Karol!" I said as she approached the security gate to the apartment complex. I shoved the shifter into park and jumped out of the Monte Carlo. "Here's your extra key."

"Vincent, where're you going, and when did you have time to pack all of your stuff? Your car is full of equipment. Where did it all come from?"

"Karol, listen—you're a very intelligent person. I'm sorry if I caused you any hurt or discomfort. But hug my son for me and continue to take care of him."

She looked stunned. "You're leaving like this?" she screamed.

"You have to excuse me, but I must, and it has to be now, though I'll keep in touch."

I reached for her arm, pulling her closer to me, and we stood locked in a loving embrace. When she finally let go, I stepped away, moving backward a few feet with my right hand feeling for the door handle of the car, leaving her standing there with what I could only imagine was an unbelievable amount of hurt. But to keep them safe, I had to leave. If there was a better option for me, it hadn't come to my attention.

I needed space because everybody had questions, questions I wasn't prepared for or willing to answer. Teresa was only a couple of hours away, and I needed a place to relax. She and I had always been close, and taking a chance on paying her a surprise visit was one

I didn't mind taking. When her father was living, it was a home I could always visit and feel welcome.

I'd done a lot while there in New York. Most of it wasn't good, and from the looks of things, everybody seemed to be aware of it. There was only one thing for me to do. I peeled away in the Monte Carlo and headed to Cherry Hill.

The trip seemed much longer than usual, but the farther behind me New York appeared to be, the more relaxed I became. Finally, I was there in my old stomping grounds, and I pulled up to the curb right in front of Teresa's jewelry store.

Approaching the store with a smile, I pulled open the door, walked in, and stood to the left of her register. It had been over three years since we'd seen each other last, down in Atlanta, Ga.

"Vincent, is that you?"

"Who'd you think it was? A ghost?"

"Man, what are you doing here?"

"Truthfully..."

"No, Vincent. That's okay! Just tell me how long you can stay."

"A few days... Just finished a couple of schools in New York. Needed some time to relax before heading down south." It was all I could tell her. What was really going on, she didn't need to know. Things had gotten ugly, and the less said, the better.

"Great timing. I'm headed to Atlantic City for the weekend with family from my father's side. Would you like to come?"

She was beautiful, standing there behind that register and looking like a fresh lily in full bloom. She had me blushing. Seeing her so happy also had me smiling! I realized smiling was something I hadn't been doing a lot of lately.

"Certainly. I'd love to join you. First, I got-ta find a room and get cleaned up. I'll meet with you later."

"A room? No way! The key to the guest house is in Daddy's shop, the same place as when he was here. Get some rest, and I'll see you after work."

***

We all finally met at the Mayflower Hotel in Atlantic City, and after finding our way to the beach, the entire group had the most joyous time building sandcastles and burying one another until we could hardly see any body parts. We continued clowning with joy and laughter as though we were a bunch of kids until deciding to settle down at Nathan's Famous for an evening snack. That turned out to be way more than just a snack. Each plate was loaded. No matter the entrée—bacon cheddar cheesy burger, beef and cheesy loaded hotdog, or the famous loaded cheesy fries, bets were placed on who could finish their entire meal, a wager none of us came close to winning. It was truly a pleasure meeting Teresa's family from Puerto Rico, and it made for a splendid, relaxing weekend with plenty of laughter. Forgetting everything that was going on for the past few days had been unthinkable before.

Unfortunately, the weekend had come to an end, and reality started to creep back to the forefront. It was time to head out.

"Hey, Vincent, will you be going by Valarie's car lot when you return to Cherry Hill?"

"Actually, Teresa, I hadn't given it a thought."

"Valarie and Agent would love to see you. Man, you wouldn't believe how well she's doing. Agent has turned the car lot into one of the best small businesses in town. I can't believe what you did for her and your friend Agent, especially sitting with him through his drug rehab. Then helping to set them up in business like you did... you were like a rolling angel back then. You must go visit."

I couldn't see doing that, with my conscience eating at me from the *guilt* of leaving Karol and my son the way I did. It wasn't right,

192

and I knew it, but from the pressure I was feeling at the time, I had no other choice.

It was now Wednesday evening, the twenty-ninth of June, and I knew the problem facing me couldn't be avoided. But before I could decide about any of that, and about Moke and the others, I had to be brave. No matter what the consequences were, Karol needed a reason for me leaving that way. As for visiting Agent or any of the others, I didn't have time for that, my head was finally clear.

Heck, New York is the largest darn city in the country. It's over ten million people, and I'm just one of them, like a needle in a haystack. I decided to call, knowing it would be asking a lot of her to take a trip to Michigan with me, though it would probably mean a lot to her, considering the way I left. If leaving that way was bothering me, I could only imagine what it was doing to her.

She deserved better, and I needed to show it to her.

"Hello?"

"Karol, I know it's a little late, and I can't go into no long conversation, but I'll be back in the city Friday evening. Could you pack some stuff and have our son ready to ride over to Flint, Michigan, with us? I'd like for you to spend some time with my sisters for the weekend."

"Vincent, where are you, and why did you leave like that?"

"I can't explain right now. Just be ready to leave once I get there Friday."

"What time, Vincent?"

"I'll be there around five p.m."

"Okay, but don't you lie to me."

"Don't worry, I'll be there. Just be ready at five."

Then suddenly a thought crossed my mind. Ms. Whitley's claim was a cop wanted to speak with me at the investigation school. *Well, for right now, forget a damn cop. I'm going back. If the cops need to speak to or question me, they will have to wait.*

And what Mrs. Tyler spoke about at the modeling school... that could wait, too. Heck, she told me John Paul could hardly see, couldn't talk, and could barely breathe, so it didn't appear he would be a threat to them anyway. *Like I said, forget everybody for right now. I'm taking the rest of the week, and we are going to Flint. Once I return, then I'll get Moke from Brooklyn and we'll make our way to South Carolina.*

***

Thursday, the next morning, my guilty conscience stood fast, Agent was my best friend. I called to see if he would meet me at his favorite breakfast shack for coffee. After sharing a great meal with him, we capped it off with a memorable conversation. We were about to part ways, but not before Agent opened up to me. "Vincent, before we split, I'd like to say—you've been one hell of a friend, and I'll always be grateful to you."

"Dang, Agent, where did that come from? You're not going anywhere, are you?"

"No! It's just that you disappear so much, and this was a great opportunity to let you know how I feel."

"Heck! Man, you're a much better friend than I could ever be. You keep taking care of yourself."

***

"Hello!" my sister said into the receiver.

"Cine, is this you?"

"Yes, Vincent! Where are you?"

"New Jersey, but I'm planning to come over there for the weekend. Will you guys be home?"

"Sure. When will you get here?"

"Saturday morning... Me, Karol, and DeVaan."

194

"Sounds great. We'll be looking out for you guys."

***

Finally, I peeled away from the breakfast shack, with time clearly favoring my drive. Later that evening, I pulled into Jersey City and with time to spare I rented a room for the night. The next evening, I eased into Queens, not really giving a damn about anything else but picking them up and pointing that Monte Carlo toward Flint, Michigan.

In view of it all and taking everything into account, that trip to see my sisters was the first of any kind we'd taken together as a family. After arriving in Flint, we spent a wild weekend of laughter with plenty of fun. It gave us a chance to share what had been needed—some personal family time, something we had not enjoyed the whole while we had been together. Spending time with my sisters and their families was the greatest idea I could have thought of. The time spent and pictures taken with them were something we could cherish for a lifetime.

It was now the Fourth of July. Everyone was preparing for a family day of fun and games and an evening barbeque. The next day, we planned an early morning trip to Cedar Point amusement park in Sandusky, Ohio, wanting to give DeVaan every bit of family fun we could on that trip. With that decision, we said our goodbyes to everyone early that next morning and headed out to Interstate 75. Not only did it feel great going there, we all had the most marvelous time together. In fact, things went so well that my leaving New York the way I did never appeared to bother Karol again.

After that big day, we were ready to leave for New York. Both of them were totally exhausted. Karol and DeVaan slept continuously throughout the whole night of an eight hour return trip, to Queens. The next morning after getting some much need rest, I'd try it all over again. I had explained to both of them that I would be leaving

195

early that morning, and before DeVaan was awake, Karol and I came to a mutual understanding about my departure. Afterward, all she wanted was for me to drop him off at his aunt Iola's house on my way out of town, neither of us realizing at the time that her request to me would be the last.

As Karol prepared for work, I kissed her goodbye for the last time. We never hooked up or wrapped arms around one another again until we met at the Pete Maravich Assembly Center for our granddaughter's graduation from LSU in June of 2023. Nearly fifty years later, she, my wife, and I took a lovely picture together.

***

It was time for me to face my troubles, but before doing that and while dropping DeVaan off, I wanted to step inside just for a minute to holler at Iola.

Once we made it to her place, I knocked, and a second later, the door opened.

"Hey, y'all!" she greeted us. "Come in! How was the trip?"

"It was great, Aunt Iola," DeVaan answered as he stepped inside. "We had a good time."

"Hey, Iola!" I said. "Can I holler at you in the kitchen?"

"DeVaan, go put your stuff in the bedroom. Yes. What is it, Vincent?"

"This is it for me. I'm leaving New York today. Karol already knows. She's as strong as they come, but please continue looking in on her and DeVaan."

"Vincent, they will be fine. She's my little sister."

"Thanks. Hopefully, I'll see you in the future."

"Take care of yourself."

With no hard feelings and no regret, I felt good about myself, knowing I was leaving them safe. All of what I had done over the past week and through the weekend was taking a big chance, but that was okay because the only thing that really mattered was them.

With my thoughts twirling around in my head, the walk back to the car seemed extra-long.

***

It had come time to pick Moke up. I had not only put off the others who wanted to question me, but him as well. Delaying everybody for the past week left little time to get in touch with him, something that needed my immediate attention. Meeting in Brownsville at his granny's house would be risky and not very smart, and honestly, I didn't care to go back. Two people had been murdered within the same week, one on each side of his granny's house. Obviously, something had gone wrong over there. Nevertheless, I needed to reach out to him, but how? Then I thought... The security guard station would be perfect, I need to holler at Ali anyway.

Plus, getting in contact with Moke Sr. before heading south was also extremely important. I for damn sure didn't want to run into the middle of a staged police trap of some kind. Detective Moke would not have called if there wasn't anything wrong. What could it be, though? Hell, Ali wanted to purchase a hundred of those Dilaudids at twenty-five bucks each. I could take care of that and make the call, too. My dude already knew the potency of the pill, so I decided to park out of the way and walk back to Lefrak City.

"Ali." I called quietly. "What-up?" He said. "I have your package. Is that lick still on? I asked. "Yeah, is the cap still the same at twenty-five?" He asked. "Sure."

"Then here's the phone, cause, I know that's not the only reason you're here."

"My dude!" I said with a smile.

Chapter 30. Moke's Safety

"Sergeant Moke, please. Is he in?"

"Sergeant!" the person called out.

"Can I help you?"

"Mr. Moke, it's Vincent. I've been told you needed to speak with me."

"Yes, and clearly there was a problem in getting the message to you. That was over a week ago."

"No, sir. That wasn't it at all. Not only did I get the message to call you, but I was told to do so right away. Please excuse me if I wasn't able to follow up. My immediate attention was needed, and I was headed out of town when you called. But for any inconvenience or delay I may have caused, sir, I apologize."

He opened up with a conversation concerning Pastor Bryant, explaining the truth about his friend. He had gotten his pastor to admit to the church that he had an uncontrollable drug addiction. He also stated the pastor was willing to take time off to be evaluated in order to assess his situation. In return for his confession, the church would be forgiving, on the condition he admitted himself into rehab. Faithfully, he did, and it was something that changed him into a different man.

He then continued with the real reason for the call, and believe me—it was a bit more serious than the pastor getting himself straight. He asked if I knew anything about Moke Jr. selling pills in his mother's neighborhood. He had been told the pills were making people sick, and a couple of them had overdosed and almost died because of the drug's potency. People had no idea how to use whatever his son was supposed to have been distributing.

Man, those pills are worth a hundred dollars apiece. Moke's been sitting on two thousand of them, and he's not the type to make a sale. But could this have something to do with those murders on Moke's grandmother's block? Dang! I hope not. He was supposed to have sat on those in case times got tough on us. Now it's clear why he's so edgy and anxious to get the hell out of Brooklyn.

"Mr. Moke, to answer your question—no, sir! I'm not aware of him selling any pills." *Wow! This is the second time this has been mentioned to me.*

"Okay, Vincent, one other thing—do you know a Detective Staten from the OCPD?"

"Yes, sir. I've met 'em briefly. What about 'em?"

"Son, he has a rap sheet on you that stretches about a mile long. I don't get how you can be on the streets."

I decided not to defend myself with Sergeant Moke, given Officer Staten's report. His precinct seemed to have more information about my past criminal history than I did. Looking back, I didn't see how a personal rap sheet on me could possibly be so extensive. If memory served me correctly, I'd only been arrested three times in my adult life, not enough to comprise a mile-long list. What they had were reports of crimes I was *supposed* to have committed, and I didn't care how many there were. The last I'd read, it didn't matter how many times I'd been picked up for questioning. They weren't registered as bookings, nor were they considered arrest reports.

"Mr. Moke, can I ask you something?"

"Sure, feel free because it seems like freedom is something you'll soon be without."

"How did Detective Staten find you?"

"Vincent, do you remember leaving South Carolina, when you said to me, 'Sir, I can't tell you everything, but I'll tell you what I can'? Well, it's the same for me this time, and you wouldn't get help at all if it weren't for my son. Young man, I don't know what your problem is, but you can't outsmart everyone. Sooner or later, you'll be stopped, and I pray that my son is not with you."

"Don't worry about that, sir. He's my friend, and I would only try to protect him as I would do for myself. He isn't doing anything that I know of, and just as soon as I can reach him, we'll make our preparations to head your way."

"Good, Vincent, because I'm told from a very reliable source you could possibly be the leader of a group who cashed a series of money orders there in New York. Would you know anything about that?"

"No. I know nothing about a group, sir, nor do I know anything about any money orders cashed in New York. If I may ask, sir—from whom are you getting this information?"

"I can't tell you any of that, but what I can say is that they are in several places around you. You must be careful, and you can quit telling me you know nothing. Listen to me—I suggest you get out of New York."

"Sir, I'm listening, and I'll ask again—where is all this coming from?"

"Son, that's irrelevant, but Moke has a cousin who works for the NYPD, and when our last name came across his workload and surveillance report, it caught his eye. Unfortunately, he was able to do some research, and according to his findings, it was none other than my only son, Moke Jr."

"Why would the cops have a surveillance on Moke when he hasn't done anything?"

"Vincent, it's been brought to our attention that a couple of people have been murdered on the block where my son is living with his grandmother. Several have overdosed to near death from the use of a certain pill being sold there. Vincent, my son's name surfaced as the primary distributor of those pills. It has also come up that he's been selling five-dollar marijuana joints in Washington Square Park. So, all of this is considered nothing to you?"

"Sir, it's not what you think! He's not selling marijuana joints, as you claim, and as for the pills, I'm almost positive he wouldn't be anybody's primary distributor. He's not that type, sir."

"Vincent, whether you're convinced of that or not, selling marijuana or not, having any of these items in his possession is still wrong."

"That would be true, sir, but possession of a single joint is only a misdemeanor in this state. All you get is a ticket and a fine."

"Vincent, I see you've done your homework, and I don't know if you had anything to do with Moke pushing those pills or not. But you can consider us even... Saturday morning before daylight, I'll have my nephew grab Moke from his grandmother's and meet you at the Newark International Airport pickup lane around five o'clock in the a.m. Whatever you do, do not go into Brownsville for any reason. It's very doubtful that you'd make it out. I'll be looking for you no later than nine o'clock Sunday morning, and be prepared to watch your friend's baptism."

Mr. Moke had anger in his voice, but for the sake of his son, he was giving me a chance to leave New York. Whether he felt the authorities had enough to finally make an arrest or not, he was willing to let me go in return for his son. True, Moke was ready to leave New York more than anything, but he wanted us to leave together. We had real love for one another, and I understood his love rope was breaking in half. He had come to realize he'd had enough of the way I lived, and my lifestyle wasn't for him. I could also tell he wanted to see me alive once we departed. My intent was to never tell him about John Paul and his beating to near death. The way I saw it, being the son of a cop, he had experienced more than enough. "Sure, sir. No problem. I'll have him there."

"Vincent, before we hang up, I suggest you find another profession. These people will soon catch up to you. Glancing at your track record, it'll be years before you see the outside of a prison yard.

Why are you going to school if you're not going to benefit from what you learn?"

Mr. Moke made me feel like a child who had badly drifted astray, with chances of survival only possible through special prayers to a higher power. He'd discovered the wrong I had done and expressed to me that it was beyond reprehensible. Mr. Moke also explained that there wasn't a conversation to be had that would change who I was—that was up to me.

He said not to go into Brownsville, and I didn't intend to, but I needed to speak with Franco before leaving. My man had a warehouse filled with weapons, and I didn't see any reason why he couldn't use a few more.

It was the post-Vietnam era. The war was over, and all the former heroes were after the M16 rifle. I hadn't spent much time at Franco's warehouse, but enough to notice there wasn't a single military rifle. Known fact—guys were prone to hug and sleep with those weapons every night for months straight while fighting the war. Most, if not all, picked the M16 as the weapon of choice in protecting their family, and from my understanding, guys were willing to pay top dollar for a solid M16 with all the accessories, especially a black-market weapon, one with no trace of ownership.

At the time he said it, I didn't quite understand what Franco meant by his statement that it was better to listen than to speak. Be that as it may, the statement carried a significant amount of clout. Listening to Sonny a while back explaining how he was sitting on over twenty automatic machine guns, I listened, but had I *really* listened? No. Because it never dawned on me that Sonny had implied *fully* automatic, and more than likely that meant M16s, considered the safest, most accurate weapon in the country... provided you could get your hands on one. They were not designed or intended for public use, making them almost impossible to obtain.

I figured the guns that Sonny had were worth close to forty grand or more because those M16 rifles were unloading for approximately two grand apiece at black-market costs. I imagined Franco could use some, if not all, of them. All I had to do was find out if he was interested, and if there was a possibility of some type of deal. If so, I had to figure out how to get me and the guns back to New York safely.

Yet getting word to Franco that the weapons were available was almost impossible without reaching out to him. *Shit! I never got his number, and I got-ta make this happen. I'll drive to his Bodega and explain to Julia the store clerk what my needs are.*

Closing the door after I stepped inside; I walked straight to the counter where she was just closing a sale. I then asked, "Julia is Franco here today?"

"No! Vincent. He's out of the country for a few days, is it anything I can help you with?" she asked. "Yes, it is... You're very familiar with our relationship, and I didn't get his number." I said to her. "No problem Vincent. He'd told me if you were ever to show up, to give you this box." She, then reached it to me. I open it standing there, a box of ammo for the weapon he'd given me and a note with his personal information written on it. Julia then asked, "Vincent is that what you need, is it anything else that I can help you with?" She asked cordially.

***

"Yes, Julia, could I use your phone? I need to call my friend in Brownsville."

"Sure but come on around the counter. The cord's too short to reach."

I dialed and Moke answered. "Hey man, is everything still on for Saturday morning?"

"Yeah, Vincent. Have you made it back from Michigan yet?"

"Don't worry about me. I'll be there."

"Oh, there's been a change, Vincent. My cousin won't be able to bring me. He has a friend who's picking me up."

"No problem." I was told not to go into Brownsville, and I had no intention of doing so. It was only Wednesday, the sixth of July. I could get a room in Newark for a couple of days and wait for Moke to arrive at the airport.

***

Dammit! It was Saturday morning, well after five a.m., and I was just pulling into the airport's pickup lane, having overslept. I expected that everybody was sitting nervously, wondering if I would show up. I didn't see Moke the first time past the terminal, as he had laid back in his seat, and I wasn't aware of the type of vehicle they were in.

They must have spotted the Monte Carlo because Moke had gotten out of the car and was standing next to it my second time around. I also noticed two men sitting in a vehicle several cars in front of the one Moke was in. The one behind the wheel looked to be Korey, the classmate who had approached me at school a little while back, the one with his cap turned backward. *Heck! This doesn't look good.*

I stopped briefly to advise them I'd be making a third pass. "Moke, listen close. Give me ten minutes. Once I return, I'll need your help. I can't explain much right now, no more than I'll blow my horn once I get close to you. There's a car ahead of you with a classmate of mine sitting in it. I'm going to block that car in. But first I got-ta get a vehicle to do it with. Like I said earlier, I'll blow my horn when I return. Whatever you do, don't tell the guy you're riding with what we're doing, only that you need him to pull out once you hear the horn and remember to have him stop right ahead of that third vehicle. When I'm done blocking them in, I'll run to you and

204

climb into the back seat. Then your boy can carry us to where I've left the Monte Carlo, and we can get going."

"Vincent, getting him to move out of the lane and to park ahead of the third vehicle is one thing, but what if he refuses to carry us to your car?"

"True, Moke! And something doesn't seem right, but don't worry. He will."

"What-ta you mean?"

"Just do what I ask. I'll be right back."

He stepped away from the car and I drove slowly, looking for anybody else who looked suspicious.

Heck, I used most of my ten minutes deciding where to leave the Monte Carlo. The least of my worries was finding a vehicle to *take*. I finally got one, hotwired it, and returned to the passenger pickup lane, blowing the horn as I came to a stop no more than a couple of feet behind them. The guy pulled out and parked in front of the third vehicle, just as Moke directed him to do.

I continued driving behind them and parallel parked next to the car Korey was in. He couldn't get out of his parking spot and no one else could come through the pickup lane. I left the car in the middle of the road, leaving that area in front of the airport completely blocked. I took a look at Korey's car, but there was no way to tell who the person with him was.

"What up, my man? Just follow the exit signs," I said, leaning over the front seat, M1911 pistol in hand. I had no intention of using it, but I needed his vehicle to move, and quickly. "I'll tell you when to stop."

Believe me, that delay gave us the opportunity we needed to completely lose them. I wasn't sure why Korey would be at the airport's pickup lane at the same time we were. My first thought was it had something to do with Juncos, but for whatever reason, whether coincidence or he and Juncos working together, I wasn't chancing it. I'd been suspicious of him from the day we met.

When Moke looked over and saw Korey, he seemed shocked. "Vincent!" he yelled. "That was Korey. Why did you block him in?"

"Moke, who in the hell is Korey, and how do you know him?"

He went on to tell me Korey was from his neighborhood in Brownsville, and they were good friends. I quickly grabbed Moke by his shoulder. "Man, are you sure of this?"

"Yes! We're only a few blocks apart."

"Okay, well, do you know this guy Korey and I are at the same school? Matter of fact, Moke, he just tried purchasing drugs from me a couple of weeks ago."

"No, I didn't know, but what are you getting at, Vincent?" He was speaking loudly and very abruptly, not understanding what I was telling him.

Man, my mind clicked, *had Juncos gotten that close to me?* "Stop the car. Let us out. The Monte Carlo's right there. Grab the rest of your stuff, Moke. I'll take this bag with me." It had the remainder of the marijuana sticks, the Dilaudids, and the money that was made from it all, including the three-card monte scheme.

After saying whatever words of goodbye to his cousin's friend (no idea if that guy had a clue what just happened), Moke returned to the car, threw his bags in the back seat, and we were off.

South Carolina was looking pretty damn good at that juncture.

***

Noticing Korey sitting in that pickup lane validated my suspicion of him, but never would I have guessed *Moke* was the reason he was there.

"Moke, this dude can't be who you think he is. What is he after? What have you done?"

He was confused after seeing me block Korey's car in, not realizing I had been warned by his father that agents could be in several places around me. With Korey popping up like that, I wasn't taking any chances.

While keeping my eye on my rearview mirror as we continued south, I asked again, "Come on, tell me what you've done."

I remembered his father mentioning his name appearing on a list for selling drugs. That seemed impossible to me, so I pulled into the next service station, reached for his bag, and opened it. I was expecting to find four different bags, each filled with five hundred Dilaudids. I should have been stunned, but after putting it all together, I began to realize why he was ready to leave.

"Moke! Where are they? What have you done with the rest of the pills?"

"I fronted a guy five hundred of them to sell for me. He did, and I got twenty-five hundred in return. He wanted another batch to do the same as before."

"What happened to this guy, Moke? How long has it been since you made this deal?"

"Over a month ago, but I haven't seen him lately, Vincent. Not since I gave him the second batch."

"Man, those pills are powerful. They'll hurt people, Moke. You shouldn't have done that, and for only twenty-five hundred dollars? Man, you could have gotten that for just fifty of those pills. Though that's beside the point. Have you spoken with your dad lately?"

"Yeah! But only about my cousin who was coming to take me to the airport. I'm sure he doesn't know what I've done. Otherwise, he would have mentioned it."

"Yes, you're probably right. More than likely, he doesn't know."

I think he knew the trouble he had caused, but not to its full extent. For some reason, his father chose not to mention anything to him, so I followed his lead. The guy Moke fronted those pills to must have gotten busted and been forced to share information with Korey. Because soon as those pills hit the streets, people were nearly dying from overdoses, and from what his father had told me, if any were to die, this guy would be charged with their death.

After listening to Moke explain what he had done, I put it together with what his father had told me. His nephew who worked for the NYPD was, I believe, also working with Korey. I believe Korey was also working with Juncos because nobody knew Moke was going to be picked up at his granny's but his father, his cousin, and me, making it almost impossible for Korey to know, and I never laid eyes on the passenger, who could have been Juncos. They must have followed him from the neighborhood, waiting for that one opportunity to catch us together.

This was one Moke had pulled over on me, trying to make himself feel bigger than he was. It worked for a little while, but he had put everyone around him at risk by making people think he was the new dealer who could get that one drug everybody was after.

As much of a scare as that turned out to be, I couldn't be angry at Moke. I was trying to be understanding and sympathetic, as he had been surrounded by all types of illegal drugs and drug trafficking that took place in his neighborhood. He just wanted to be a part of something exciting.

Spartanburg was a little less than twelve hours away. After we got rolling again, we'd only stop to get gas. Even though I was expecting our arrival at Moke's house to be slightly earlier than planned, I had already made the decision not to witness the baptism.

"Hey, dude!" I said to him. "Wake up!"

"Where are we?"

"At the corner store down the street from your parents' house. Dang, you must have really gotten relaxed. You've slept for hours. And if you were to snore once more, I was going to put your ass out of this car."

"Gosh, Smooth, I'm surprised you didn't get a ticket. You must've been flying."

"Smooth! Huh. Man, that's only the second time I've ever heard you call me that."

"I know. I prefer Vincent."

"I was moving fast, but not enough to donate to your state treasury fund again. Look, there's no one expecting us here this early. We have a few minutes to spend together, though we can't overdo it, being so close to your house. Listen, once I'm gone, I need for you to call your dad to come get you."

Moke seemed to understand. "It's only a couple blocks, and the bags aren't very large. I can walk. Anyway, once I'm home, no one will know exactly how long you've been gone."

"Vincent, I would like to say—from that first day you invited me to lunch, I've always held a deep affection and love for you."

"Moke, the feeling is mutual." We embraced in a great hug. "This is it," I said, and we continued to hug until I started to weaken.

"Look man, I don't know if this is against the town's ordinance, but if we don't stop, we just may be arrested for obscenity."

We both pushed away, and he asked, "Will you be all right?"

"I think so."

"Then get out-ta here before you're noticed."

With that, I hopped into the driver's seat. The motor was still running, and I pulled the shifter to drive and eased off, looking back at Moke. I was probably safe, but no way was I taking the chance of getting caught in South Carolina. No one other than his cousin should have known about the early morning drop-off at the Newark airport. I'll never know for sure, but after seeing Korey in that car, I'll always believe his father never intended for me to make the trip to South Carolina with his son.

Chapter 31. Preparing for the Weapons

After bringing the Monte Carlo to rest in Greenville, South Carolina, where no one knew me, and Spartanburg was far enough behind for me, I could relax with confidence. I needed some rest, so I pulled into a rest area and went to sleep in the back seat of the car.

The next morning, I got up, walked to the restroom, and took a thorough and complete cowboy wash, including brushing my teeth. Afterward, I left feeling fresh and great about myself, and I couldn't think of anything better than grabbing a wonderful meal at Stax's Original Restaurant, where I could slice and dice some of the best country ham in the world. Just the thought of an Appalachian style breakfast was making me hungry.

The phone booth wasn't busy. There was only one using it and one person waiting. But once it appeared that I was coming to use it, everyone sitting or standing around the area gathered behind that one person as if they were all waiting to use it... or to make a statement that it was for Whites only.

Damn! What the fuck just happened? I'll have to make these calls later. Hopefully, this shit doesn't follow me up the street 'cause I'll have to pass on getting my country ham sliced and diced and then find a phone booth that's not so occupied.

No, the only thing that followed me was probably an emotionally traumatic experience. Maybe Greenville's phone booth incident reminded me of some unrelated event from back home, a mental flashback to the all-White phone booths of the past.

After entering Stax's for breakfast that morning, I never gave another thought to what happened or to the idea I could've been followed by several of those individuals. Once the door was closed behind me, I was immediately seated and offered a cup of coffee, a glass of water, and a lovely breakfast menu.

"Are you ready to order, sir?" the friendly server asked.

I was stunned as hell by their warm service. "Yes," I finally managed, my head nodding up and down rapidly. "I'm starving."

"Then you'll need our big breakfast special," suggested the friendly waitress. "It's a large slice of country ham topped with two over-easy eggs and covered with a special house blend of melted cheese. You also get a side of chunky scalloped potatoes, soft buttered pancakes served with a jar of hot maple syrup, and a tall glass of freshly squeezed orange juice. How does that sound to you?"

"Delicious, I must say," I answered, having completely forgotten the phone booth incident.

When I finally slid my chair from the table to leave Stax's Original Restaurant, I could hardly stand. I was full... filled both with a sensational amount of tasty food and thoughts of the restaurant's hospitality, which was incomparable.

***

After hopping over to Anderson, South Carolina, and finding a phone booth that wasn't as engaged, I proceeded with those calls. I realized my last conversation with Natalie was over two months ago. I had gotten so wrapped up in everything, I couldn't find time to reach out to her. It was also getting close to Lola's graduation. Our trip to Flint was nearing, so keeping in touch was a must.

Also, even though Sonny previously informed me about the weapons, I had to find out their present status.

"Sonny!"

"Yeah. Is this you, Smooth?" he asked, sounding like he was anxious to hear from me.

"Yeah, I've been wanting to get back to you, but things been getting in the way. Hey, I do have a few quick questions for you."

"What is it? You caught me on break."

"Cool. We're both pressed for time, but how many of those pieces can you muster up?"

"I didn't think that you were interested, but right now, I have over thirty of them."

"Over thirty! Damn!"

"Twenty-two of those are M16s, the fully automatic machine gun."

My first thought was, *What the hell could I do with that many guns?* Thinking quickly that I would already be close to Kansas, I decided I should contact Bru Boy once my conversation was over. It certainly couldn't hurt.

That proved true when I found out he was interested in relieving me of five sets of weapons, including five 1911 handguns, and he only questioned me about the cost of the five M16s. Mostly because of their low cost, he needed to know the weapons were faultless. I assured him of that and noted he would be getting them ahead of black-market cost. The war had ended, and the M16 had replaced the previous weapon used by the armed forces, making it valuable and unlawful to own and causing the cost to rise extremely high for those who were able to find one. Bru Boy was willing to pay nine grand for the ten weapons with no problem. If only it would go that well with Franco back in Brooklyn.

My call to Franco turned out to be very productive, as he explained the amount of risk involved in moving around as much as I did alone. He had so many friends who had died needlessly. They had been careless in their talk and actions and had never learned how to operate in silence. That got them in trouble they couldn't get out of. But he was glad to hear I was okay and had gotten out of New York unharmed.

After explaining the purpose of my call, he assured me of his interest and warned me to be extra careful. Whatever type of weaponry I could produce, he would be willing to purchase, especially any type that was fully automatic, regardless of its brand or whether it was a rifle or pistol. During our brief conversation, I told Franco that I had over twenty machine guns but needed around 1,300 bucks apiece to get them to him.

"Don't worry, Vincent. Whatever you have, bring them. There's plenty of room in the warehouse. For that price, I'll take every military rifle you bring, especially the M16s. The cost of those is heading toward the clouds. If you make it happen, get back to me using this same number. In the meantime, I'll start making room for the oversized stash."

I was taken by surprise, though I shouldn't have been considering my first visit to his place, not to mention meeting Franco and his wife Carmellia that night several years back at the Harold Melvin & the Blue Notes concert. It created a special vibe, the kind you would cherish for life. It was my first date night in Philly when he offered those seats to Madelyn and me over all the others who had passed by his table. That was impressive in itself, and walking into his warehouse was just as amazing as the night he offered us those seats. So as far as being surprised at what came from Franco, I shouldn't have been. We closed out our conversation, and I continued on with my trip.

While traveling west on I-20 toward Tallulah, Louisiana, listening to Marvin Gaye's hit "Got to Give It Up," I thought, *I'm going to need help.* After noticing the sign ahead said Highway 65 South and realizing how close I was to Ferriday, La., I thought I'd stop and check with Dannie. *He'll more than likely be glad to help with these weapons. I can't do all of this work and driving alone. Once it's all over and I'm done in New York, he can fly back to Ferriday, and maybe I'll continue to Flint. But first I got-ta take Highway 65 to our hometown and take a chance that Dannie's around. It wouldn't hurt to see if he were willing to make a couple of grand for a few days of work.*

The weather was really nice, and the sky was a North Carolina blue, beautiful as ever. The T-tops were out, and the Monte Carlo's engine was in rhythm while I coasted the back roads through the cotton fields of Louisiana.

It was only a little after eight o'clock. I decided to stop by Mrs. Brierfield's to see if she could tell me where Dannie was. I really didn't have to knock. Her door was always open, and she would be sewing clothes, sometimes well into the evening.

"Mrs. Brierfield, how are you?"

"I'm good, Vincent. If you're looking for your friend, I think he's at that club across the bayou. I think it's called the Pro Toe."

"Okay. It's good to see you again, Mrs. Brierfield."

"You boys stay out of trouble now."

"Yes, Mrs. Brierfield. We will."

Sure enough, Dannie was there over the bayou at the Pro Toe club. He was standing with Peter T, running his mouth as usual, the loudest person you'd hear when you entered the bar.

He greeted me in his favorite way. "Smooth! What's up, my nickel? I love you, mon, ya-heard!"

We dapped and embraced with all the strength we had. Getting Dannie to go wasn't a problem. The dude loved adventurous and exciting trips. Actually, this was a favor I shouldn't have been asking of him because of the circumstances. He wasn't supposed to travel where I needed to go.

Then I turned and embraced another little homeboy of mine, Peter T. We too had grown up together, though we were not as close as Dannie and me. *He's more capable of doing the right thing*, I thought, staring him directly in his eyes. He was more dependable, and I thought about asking him instead, but we had never traveled together, and more importantly—his daddy was a cop. That turned my attention back to Dannie, someone I still had faith in, even if he was prone to get a little wild and wasn't supposed to travel back west. We were two of the same—neither of us gave a damn.

"Hey, Dannie!" I yelled. "Let me holler at you outside."

"What you got, my nickel?"

"How'd you like to make a couple grand really quick?"

"Shit, Smooth! How quick, and what I got-ta do?"

Dannie was a handful, but I could deal with him. Anytime he was around, a strategy of some kind had to be in place to manage his behavior. Still, he didn't bother me. We were homeboys and had known each other since we were kids. We grew up in the same alley in Ferriday, the one we called the Back of Fourth because it ran behind Fourth Street, the town's main drag.

"Just ride with me to pick something up. It should only take a few days."

"When we leaving, ya-heard?"

"Tomorrow morning at six. Meet me across the street from your house, at Billups's filling station."

"You got it! I'll be there, my nickel."

I left and spent the night with my mother in Doty Garden, our little subdivision. I never liked the name our subdivision was given, and I vowed never to live out there because of it. Still, it was always exciting watching my mother's face light up when I walked through her door. She was a very religious woman and would always give spiritual quotes when I was there. I had faith in her deliverances and could trust that they would help guide me through Satan's mischievous traps. Her house was safe for me. Hell, my whole hometown seemed safe for me, but once outside those parameters, that "It" would take control over my actions. No matter how much I wanted to stop, I couldn't find the will to conquer this evilness inside me. What I did know to be fact—my mother didn't raise me to be who I had become.

"Baby, you look tired. I got your bed all fixed just the way you like it."

We sat and talked for just a little while before turning in for the night. The next morning, I pulled out before she'd awoken to meet

Dannie. Just as promised, he was there on time at 6:00 a.m., as if he had never been asleep. At 6:20 a.m., we were headed northwest to Oklahoma.

Late that same evening of July 13, after driving for nearly eleven hours, he and I pulled in hungry and tired to the city of Edmond.

Chapter 32. Securing the Weapons

"Damn, Smooth, this shit seems weird. These people will lock me the fuck up if I'm caught out here, ya-heard!" His statement was true and getting him out probably wouldn't be easy.

"Don't worry. Nobody will know. We'll only be here for a few days. My understanding is that everything is already secured and packaged. All we have to do is rent a U-Haul to transport this shit, pay for the product, and get the hell out of here. Just don't do anything stupid that will get us in trouble, and be cool in the damn barrooms, especially that club Tike's."

"I gotcha. Once I'm settled into the hotel, I'll get in touch with Newt. When you get ready to take care of business, just let me know."

It was risky leaving Dannie to himself after his previous scare there with the cops, though I felt strongly it would be fine.

Getting in touch with Lola had become important because soon the both of us would be headed to Flint. I didn't care if we had no job or place to live. I'd figure that shit out once we arrived. Getting her away from her family in Arkansas was my largest obstacle, but I would leave it to her.

Lola had moved into a smaller apartment, and after catching up to her there, I explained that we would meet at her parents' house after finals in a few weeks. She was excited about moving to Flint, even though she didn't know the true reason for it. I had a plan, a scheme and Lola I thought would work perfect for what my intentions were. A revenge... My only problem would be keeping her happy, while trying to pull her into my secrete scheme. I owed the city of Flint, Michigan from the way those cops had previously treated me there—this revenge was a long time coming, and I had no control of the "It" that was driving me.

After spending as much time with Lola as I could, I turned my attention to Sonny. I needed to get those weapons and have them loaded. Figuring in the travel fee back to New York, plus the two grand I had offered Dannie for his help, all of it was coming to around fourteen thousand dollars for the thirty weapons.

The deal I made with Franco in Brooklyn kept me from having to get back in touch with Bru Boy in Kansas City. Because Franco had agreed to purchase the entire stash, all I had to do was get them there.

"My dude, Sonny M!"

"Mr. Smooth. I wasn't sure you'd make it. How was the trip?"

"It went well, considering the distance and having to travel with Dannie. Heck, I'll tell you, like Tony the Tiger would say—Grrreat! If only this transaction goes the same."

"Cool. Are you ready to look at what I have?"

"Sure, but how were you able to get them out of inventory?"

"Man, by paying close attention to what I was taught. You left me with those forms, and I ran copies of them. Afterward, I used them to ship the damaged weapons in the place of the good ones. I also rented a storage bin from that same place you showed me, and when the time came, I could gradually transport them."

I was really impressed with what he had accomplished.

"You ready to make the trip?" Sonny asked as we walked toward his gold-colored Datsun 280Z.

"Yeah, but don't you think we should settle on the cost before we go out there?"

"It's no change. Ten and one makes it eleven grand for the thirty weapons. Five hundred each for the rifles, and one hundred apiece for the pistols."

"Well, Sonny, there will be a change. I'll give you twelve and two. Fourteen grand for the thirty weapons, and I also brought Dannie to help us load them."

"That'll work, but wasn't he told to never show up here again?"

"True, but we'll be out-ta here in a day."

"Hey, will you have time to holler at your girl Natalie?"

"Shit, dude! It's funny you asked. I'm spending the night with her, and tomorrow Dannie and I will wrap up everything. The morning after, we'll head out of here. I have to get these weapons up to New York."

"You and Lola still making that trip to Michigan?"

"Sure. It's all set in stone."

"Cool. Well then, come on. Let's go take a look at what you'll be traveling with."

Once we made it to the storage unit he started to explain the history of the weapons and their functions. "Smooth, these M16s are pretty cool. They all come with twenty-round clips. But to be safe, it's better if you only load the clip with seventeen rounds. The .45 millimeters are quite heavy. The ten pistols are all Colt 1911A1s and are hand fitted for easy use. They're also pretty cool and come with an eight-round clip, and they, too, are already packed, one for each weapon."

"Okay. Tomorrow evening, we'll get them loaded and get a good night's rest. Before dawn, we'll be gone."

***

I must say, everything went well. Getting the rental may have been our biggest issue, trying to convince U-Haul to rent us a small one-way truck to New York. After a lengthy discussion and offering some extra cash, we were finally approved. At that point, we were ready to get them loaded.

That evening, we both showed up on time, with Dannie doing the lion's share of the loading. He was about six feet and close to two hundred pounds, so loading the weapons wasn't a bother for him.

"Hey, Sonny—here's your fourteen thousand dollars. Don't spend it all in one place."

"Don't worry, Smooth! We're not like you. Money is hard to come by for most of us. Dude, the way you run the country, it's like you digging it out of the ground."

We shared a smile and a little giggle. "You got jokes, huh?"

Afterward, we returned to the hotel, where Dannie and I had a nightcap, several for me and even more for him, from what I could remember, before calling it a night.

The next morning, after getting some well-deserved rest, Dannie and I took off in the U-Haul for New York City, he in the passenger's seat with a thermos half-filled with coffee and the other half with Wild Irish Rose.

Shit. This is going to be one hell of a trip.

Off to the city we went—me, a damn drunk partner, and thirty automatic machine guns.

Dannie's help was needed, but not being able to control what he loved was difficult and very aggravating at times. Trying to discover different methods of dealing with him had become somewhat challenging. Knowing drinking and driving would be a problem, instead of me trying to stop his actions, I did the bulk of the driving. Dannie figured a hot toddy after a heavy bout of alcohol consumption would cure his hangover and keep his body sober. Maybe it did, but it didn't keep him from falling asleep, and after a full tank of gas had been consumed by the U-Haul truck, he finally awakened.

"Damn, dude!" I said. "Are you still sucking air over there? Man, I thought our next stop would be at the darn emergency room."

For several hours, Dannie had fallen into a light coma. After a full recovery, our journey to New York continued, with both of us sharing the wheel.

After nearly two days of traveling and with nothing major happening in between, we were finally in New Jersey across the river from New York. Time to find a phone.

"Franco!"

"Yeah, Vincent. Where are you?"

"Across the bridge, west of the Hudson River. Is there a specific time you'd like these to be brought into the city?"

"No, but if you were to start over the river with them now, by the time you get here, it'll be perfect. Bring them, and I'll be waiting for you. Oh, by the way—your package is ready."

"The full amount?"

"Yes. Twenty-eight thousand, as promised. Just get here. I'll see that you have a way to the airport, and don't worry about the truck. It'll be covered, too."

Later, as Dannie and I helped Franco unload the truck at his warehouse, he turned and said to me, "Vincent, you are one of a kind. Always remember—trust no one!"

Franco was sounding really serious with another one of his quotes, spoken in that deep Brooklyn accent, a distinguished underground sound that left me stunned and with not a clue about what he meant. Because I'd never considered myself different. I understood about the trust, though, because I'd let my guard down on that part. When we arrived in Brooklyn and pulled into his warehouse, I realized at that point, I had put Dannie and myself in harm's way by trusting Franco. I should have at least left Dannie a way out in case something went wrong. The way I had been thinking was terrible, trusting that Franco's prominence in the city was large and what we were doing for him was too small for anything to happen to us. Evidently, he didn't see it that way and was reminding me to be more cautious in my dealings.

"Vincent, people are not all fair. You should be careful of your environment and actions at all times. Flatbush is not congested like Manhattan and may seem not to be as dangerous, but you should treat every situation as a risk. This is still Brooklyn, and I can only secure your safety to LaGuardia. You'll be on your own after that."

Franco had planned for Dannie and me to be picked up and carried to the airport. All I had left to accomplish was making sure we both departed New York safely.

***

That turned up quickly to be a problem, soon after we boarded the plane. Dannie had created a disturbance, complaining about the size of the liquor shots and how much they were willing to let him consume. It then registered—in my travel bag, sitting in my lap, was twenty-eight thousand dollars and a small matchbox full of mixed pills I'd received from Logan. The only thing I could think of was to drop one of Logan's laboratory made Thiopens into Dannie's drink while his rampage continued.

It worked perfectly. Within fifteen minutes, he was fast asleep, and he didn't wake up until hours later when the bell sounded, and the stewardess instructed us to please buckle our seatbelts and prepare for landing. We were approximately twelve minutes from arrival. Dannie had slept through the entire trip. He really was a handful, but finally we landed, found our way to the Monte Carlo, and uneventfully made our way back to Ferriday.

Chapter 33. Visiting Natalie

It was a beautiful Saturday morning a week later, on the twenty-third of July, and my mind was set solely on getting a chance to visit Natalie in Baton Rouge, but not before I caught myself pulling into Taunton's Superette, which was right off the highway. I had just left my mother's house and was traveling Route 84 east into Ferriday, and there was no better time than now to service the Monte Carlo. While doing so, I figured it wouldn't hurt to snack on a delicious rollover sandwich. Taunton's served them several different ways, hot link, mild sausage link and of course hot Cajun style with catsup and hot sauce rolled between one slice of bread. Topped with a honeybun, and a small chocolate milk to wash it down.

It was the last Saturday of the month, and I wanted to surprise Natalie for the weekend. Once everything was taken care of with the Monte, I drove up the street to Doris's Dress Shop. There was a beautiful scarf wrapped around the neck of a mannequin, and I wanted it for her. While standing at the register, closing out a sale for a scarf identical to the one on display, I felt a tap on my right shoulder. Quickly pivoting, I saw a longtime friend who I hadn't seen for well over a year.

"Dearie! Is that you?"

"Yes, Vincent! Look at you... Man, you look to be doing well. I thought that was you pulling in back at Taunton's service station. How are you?"

"I'm decent, and you're looking great yourself." Truthfully, the compliment was meant to be uplifting, but I could tell there was something off.

"Thanks. Physically, I'm okay, but this town is about to bury me."

"Come, why don't we step outside?"

She sounded so disenchanted, so once we exited the store, I probed. "Dearie, you look rather nice. What seems to be bothering you?"

"Having nothing to do has gotten the best of me."

"Well! If I'm not mistaken from our last conversation, your intent was to go live with your father in Pontiac. What happened?"

"The opportunity never presented itself. However, I do remember that conversation. We were at the Alexandria Airport. If I remember correctly, you were going to live with your son and his mother in New York. So, what brings you home to Ferriday?"

"Passing through on my way to Baton Rouge for the weekend. I'll be back Tuesday, but then I'll be leaving for Michigan on Friday."

"To Michigan! Are you serious?"

"Yes! Leaving early Friday morning."

"Man! Is it possible you could let me ride with you?"

I didn't see any reason why she couldn't. I would be traveling alone anyway and could use the company.

"Sure, Dearie! Assuming your mother agrees, I don't see a problem with that. And providing your father knows in advance, it should be fine, though only if you're packed and ready to leave by early Friday morning 'cause I'm not waiting around."

"Don't worry about me. I'll be packed and ready before this evening has ended. But are you serious? Can I really ride with you?"

"Come on, you know me! Be packed, and I'll be by your mom's house Friday morning."

"Only one thing, Vincent—I don't have much to help with on gas."

I understood that when she mentioned the opportunity never presented itself. "Don't fret. We'll be fine. I have enough to get us there. Plus, your company will be more than enough payment because, Dearie, you never shut the heck up. Hey, I got-ta run, but look to hear from me before Friday."

"Okay! And thanks!"

"No problem, Dearie! I gotcha."

After our conversation, I pulled away from Doris's Dress Shop and headed south to Baton Rouge.

***

"Mrs. Brown, I see that you're busy today," I said, stepping into the small but crowded two-chair beauty shop. "How are you?"

Natalie's mom was taking advantage of a beautiful Saturday and appeared to be making sure all her favorite customers would be looking their best for their upcoming church service on Sunday.

"I'm doing well!" She always spoke in an incredibly low and soft tone. Having said that, on this occasion, she seemed to be more spirited than usual.

"Everyone, I would like to introduce to you my future son-in-law. This is Vincent, Natalie's friend, whom I hope one day will be the father of my grandchildren."

"Hello, Vincent," they answered in unison as I eased over to her with my arms open wide for a hug. Mrs. Brown would always kiss my forehead as we embraced, a tradition I fell in love with.

"Natalie left already."

"Where to, Mrs. Brown? Do you have any idea?"

"Yes, she's headed to the pet store. She's been saying all week there's a beautiful little puppy down there that she's fallen in love with. And you know as well as I do—when Natalie makes up her mind to do something, no one can stop her. In case she isn't there, here's the address to her new apartment. It's off Scenic Highway. Vincent, between you making it and the new puppy... darling, she'll be absolutely ecstatic."

"Thanks, Mrs. Brown!"

***

225

Out of the corner of my eye, I spotted her, standing there at the end of aisle three, but not alone. In her arms, she held the most beautiful and precious cocker spaniel puppy. It was looking extremely healthy and sporting a very shiny black coat.

She smiled when she saw me coming. "Vincent, do you like her?"

I was so amused to see them together. What could be more rewarding than petting and snuggling with the little animal?

"Nae, she's beautiful!" I said cheerfully as she continued holding her new baby close to her chest.

"She's mine, Vincent, and she's coming home with me today. Excuse me. I apologize. How are you?"

"I'm decent," I giggled. "No need to ask how you feel."

"You right... hey, look to your left. Will you grab that cage off the top shelf? I have the perfect little blanket for it, so she'll sleep comfortably the first night in her new home."

We continued to shop for other small accessories that would help please her new companion throughout the night. Natalie then approached the register, and after paying for it all, including the tiny cage I was carrying, we all departed the store, Natalie, me, and a tail-wagging bundle of joy.

"What will you name her, Natalie?"

"Hmm... I'm thinking... Misty?"

"Misty sounds excellent because she's naturally beautiful."

"Okay! I love it. Misty it is. Let's get her to my mother's shop, I'm scheduled to meet with Janelle at Ethel's Soul Food for lunch. Are you coming?"

"Sure, I haven't seen Janelle in a while. It will be a pleasure, especially while eating some good soul food at Ethel's."

***

After a magnificent meal with the two of them at Ethel's, we all departed, with the both of us continued to her mother's shop, to grabbed the little frisky pup. Afterward, we returned to her apartment, and I can assure you that it was a pleasure watching Natalie get acquainted with her little Misty.

After a splendid weekend with Nae and her mother, I found myself traveling back home, to this remarkable little town called Ferriday. At that time, it was still one of the most fascinating and entertaining blues towns in the South. As I rolled past Slick's Tire Service, I spotted my brother's little green Camaro.

"Toby!" I yelled after rolling down my window. He had gotten out of the car and was headed into Slick's. "What's going on, my lil' brother?"

"Vincent! What-ta you doing here?"

"Visiting! I was just here earlier in the week. Mama didn't tell you?"

"No! I've been away for several days. Where you coming from?"

"Baton Rouge. I went to visit Natalie for the weekend."

"Dang, dude! You really like that Natalie girl, huh?"

"Can you tell?"

"Hell, yeah! You'll blow the pistons clean out of an engine just to spend some time with her."

"Here you go with those sarcastic statements of yours."

"Call it what you want, but you love Natalie."

"Yo Toby, everyone around is calling you 'Peanut.' What's the deal with that? Does it have anything to do with that little basketball team you've started with all those kids?"

"I'm not sure, but you could say that."

"Hold up for a minute." I hopped out and gave him a hug. "Yo man, I need you to do me a favor. Could you hold a little cash for me?"

"What kind of cash? Not like once before when you had me hold those unemployment checks?"

"No! Real cash."

"Like cash money?"

"Yeah! A few thousand, Toby. Until I return?"

We happened to be standing at the side entrance of Slick's Tire Service, where you could get any type of tire repaired—bicycle, tractor, eighteen-wheeler... even a damn combine. Not only could you get your tire changed there, but Slick's was an intersection for all types of business transactions, guarded by a cruel and vicious pit bull called Spike.

Toby looked at me with his eyes sharply narrowed, index finger between his lips and thumb underneath his chin. "I guess..." he answered, suspicion streaming from his voice.

"Don't worry, Toby. It's all good." My brother was always willing to help in any way possible. He was the one individual who knew and understood his brother may be leaning somewhat toward the wrong side of the law.

He happened to be one of those who was well ahead of his time and had other things to worry about than what was going on with me. He was more focused on our mother, even though our father had returned. Though he was treating her with respect, he was still that father who traumatized us with his twisted screwups, leaving my little brother afraid to trust our mother being left alone with him.

My brother's trauma from our father's actions was way different from mine. He was as straightforward an individual as could be. Not that he was afraid our father would physically or deliberately inflict harm on our mother. At no point in our lives had either of us seen our dad be violent. He never even swore in our company. All his other antics, though... they were more than enough that my brother was not letting go of our mother, and he was just waiting for that one instance when our father would revert back to his old ways and land back in prison. The bottom line was, my brother rarely left our mother's side. In fact, he even built his workshop on her property and used her as his secretary. They were inseparable.

"No problem, Vincent! Exactly how much?" He wanted to know in case something happened and there was a discrepancy. This way, we would be on the same page.

"Thirty thousand, to be exact. And don't sweat it, Toby. I'll return in a few months."

I went on to explain I was leaving for Michigan to see if I could get one of those automotive manufacturing jobs. I heard they were paying good money just to follow a damn vehicle down an assembly line, as if they were playing tag by placing a part or two in a designated area onto a vehicle.

"Damn, Toby! Can you imagine getting paid just to attach a distributor cap and some plug wires to a motor?"

"No, I can't. It all sounds great, but I can't leave Mama here by herself."

"Dude, we all understand and appreciate what you're doing. But she'll be fine. She's surrounded by her own mother and both of her sisters. That doesn't seem to me like being left alone."

I tried to convince my brother that he should come too, but he wouldn't, and he was quick to change the subject.

"Hey, some pretty White girl dropped by a few weeks back looking for you. Kinda dressed funny but wearing the hell out of some jeans."

"What she wanted? Did she say?"

"No! Only that you two were good friends, and she needed to speak with you. Wanted to know if I could inform her of your whereabouts. Funny... I couldn't tell her if I wanted to. Gosh, man, I didn't know you had crossed over. How close are the two of you? She didn't look to be your type. Darn, big brother, I thought I knew you. Are you floating a White girl?"

"Toby, did she say at all where she was from?" I was hoping my brother had asked enough questions that I could figure out exactly who she was.

"No, though she did mention she was headed to South Carolina and if I was to hear from you anytime soon, to give you this number."

"Just this number? No name?"

"Yeah. I asked, but she said you'd know who she was. Why would a fine-ass White girl come by herself looking for you?"

Who in the heck can he be talking about? Shit! Teresa is really fine, but with more of a dark skin tone, and we were just together in Atlantic City. She wouldn't be looking for me down here. Wait... Regina? I smiled just thinking about her. *As pretty as they come. But no, Regina is more of an introvert. Too shy of a person. Never would travel such a distance alone.*

Damn, he can't be talking about Rhea. I've never seen her in anything tighter than a pair of oversized dickies. However, she's been here before and does know where I live. But I can't imagine a working Agent Collins wearing that attire.

"Dang, Toby! If she was strutting a pair of tight jeans, what else did she have on?" Rhea never wore anything but a vest, a flannel shirt, and baggy khakis.

"If you supposed to know who she is, why all the questions?"

"Because the only person with enough guts to be looking me up... she doesn't dress as you're describing. So what else was she wearing?"

"A tight, silk, gold-colored blouse. One you couldn't forget."

"A silk blouse, Toby?"

"No, I said a *tight* silk blouse. One that her breasts were trying to squeeze out of, held in by a button attached to a very weak piece of thread. And it wasn't holding on very well." He held a toothpick to his lips as he described her, mimicking blowing smoke from a cigarette.

"Was she wearing a vest over the top of her blouse?" I asked, trying to get as much information as possible. Rhea has never dressed this way.

"No, man. Why a vest? It was June, Vincent. She would burn the hell up down here wearing anything extra."

Well, that's one thing he has right, I thought as I wiped sweat from my face with a neatly folded towel. *This Louisiana heat is something to deal with.*

"Hey, hopefully this will help you—she did speak quickly with some type of northern accent."

Finally, he gave me something I could use. Rhea was from Pennsylvania, and speaking quickly was an understatement for her.

"Thanks, Toby! If it's that important, eventually she'll catch up to me. I'm headed out by Mama's. I need to spend some time with her before I leave Friday to visit our sisters."

"Okay! Tell 'em I said hello."

Chapter 34. Remembering Dearie

While traveling the back side of town toward Dearie's mother's house, I could only think of what she must have gone through to convince them to agree to such a move. It was early, way before daylight that Friday morning the twenty-ninth of July. I had only seen her once since our first meeting at Doris's Dress Shop. That was briefly at White's Grocery, a corner store down from her mother's house. It was on that conversation I based my perception that she and her parents had discussed the move, and everything had been accepted and agreed to. Every single thing, even the fact that this Friday would be her last day in Ferriday. She was confident she would never return home to live ever again.

It was amazing, though, to say the least when the time had come for us to leave, I found Dearie trying to explain what she was doing and why to her mom. I had pulled up to their house on 9th Street and found Dearie and her mother in a heated argument on the front porch. Dearie was trying to explain herself, however, her mother didn't seem exactly interested in her explanation of why she had made such a drastic decision.

Finally, Dearie came down to the car, and we looked deeply into one another's eyes. Tears were beginning to drip down her beautiful face. I could not stand to see her cry, and it was too early for me to lose my masculinity in front of her.

"What's wrong, Dearie?"

"I feel terrible. My mom doesn't understand."

"What is it she's not understanding? I'm puzzled."

"She doesn't get my reasoning for leaving this way."

I had been assured her family was okay with the plan, but no. They were not.

"Shouldn't you return? She's still standing there."

She had everyone confused and wondering—how could someone as strong and domineering as Dearie be convinced to leave with a stranger on such a long trip? It wasn't that she was going to live with her father that bothered them, but that she was leaving so suddenly with a stranger.

Unbeknownst to all concerned, we were not strangers and hadn't just met. The departure wasn't sudden, either. I'd known for a long time she wanted to leave and go live with her father in Michigan. Dearie and I had been cherishing a long-time childhood friendship with a casual love affair, all of which we kept secret. For no reason in particular, other than her mother was really strict on her girls. Therefore, Dearie's mother and sisters were confused. They didn't know me, and so they assumed I was no more than a con trying to convince Dearie to run off with me—incredibly surprising to all who knew her, considering Dearie's nature.

Maybe it was deceptive of us to keep our relationship a secret, but if she cared for me the way I thought, what difference would it make if she told her mother? I was absolutely appalled by the whole scene of her mother standing there. Consequently, my foot never moved the accelerator. Could it be the strength in my belief that the spiritual and maternal instinct within a mother has been and always will be to do what's best for a loved one? And considering who Dearie's mom was, I couldn't see her being any different.

Her mother stood firm on the front porch, her position unchanged. She needed to know, if not in-depth, at least the specifics of why her daughter was leaving with someone her family knew very little about.

"Wait here, Vincent, I'll be right back."

She returned to their porch to hold a conversation with her mother. It was dark, so there was no way I could read their lips, and I was too far off to possibly hear what was being said. But after their brief conversation, Dearie opened her arms and moved toward her mother, wrapping them around her until they were locked in a warm embrace. It sent chills through my body, even though their conversation stayed between the two of them. She returned to the Monte Carlo with a totally different vibe. Once her bags were inside and the passenger seatbelt clicked, she looked over at me.

"Let's go."

***

Getting her to Pontiac and myself to Flint had already started out in a sensitive manner. "Vincent," she muttered softly.

"Yes, what is it?"

"You've been driving for several hours in the dark. The sun's up. Aren't we close to Memphis?"

"Yeah, almost. What's up?"

"Wouldn't you like to get something to eat and afterward cruise by the motel where Dr. Martin Luther King's assassination took place? Man, there isn't anything else in the world I'd rather see right now than where he was standing when it happened."

"Sure, Dearie, and after getting something to eat, what exactly will guarantee our chances of getting close enough to see where Dr. King was standing? Do you even know the room number?"

***

Remembering all those years ago when Dr. King was assassinated...

I was a little older than Dearie, but not by much. In 1968, where he was standing when it happened wasn't something I'd formed a considerable amount of interest in. And there were great reasons for that lack of interest.

In 1968, when Dr. King was assassinated, we were fighting our own discrimination and racial battles. Students from Sevier High, where I attended which was all Black, were being chosen by the school principal and faculty during the summer to participate in a desegregation plan. They were in the process of gathering Black students who were willing to attend an all-White school, whose parents were not afraid to let them attend and were able to provide transportation, and whose GPA was at minimum strong enough to show they had the potential for completing each course with a passing grade.

The cleverness of this idea that summer of 1968 garnered a great deal of notoriety and made history for itself. With the number of Black students who attended the all-White school that year, the school was considered integrated, and following the success of what happened, our White counterparts would not stand around and accept a second year of this inflammatory behavior. Especially, after finding out in the spring of 1969 that the US Supreme Court approved final orders for desegregated school systems, throughout the entire parish to start at the beginning of the New Year. With the migration of Black students attending Ferriday High the previous year, failing to go well, for the Whites' a plan was put into play. One that would stall the Courts decision. A Plan that would provide desegregation by gender at both____ Ferriday High Schools. Calling for all boys, Black and White to attend the Ferriday High School, while sending all girls Black and White to Sevier High for the remainder of the 1969-70 school year.

Ferriday wasn't having any part of this total parish desegregated, ruling. In fact, the White people of Ferriday wasn't ready for desegregated school system. All they wanted at the moment was a protective measure that would keep Black boys away from White girls, until their secret plan could be completed, which was kept undisclosed. So, allowing the schools of Ferriday to be desegregated by gender for the remainder of the 1969-70 school year, sending all Boys to the White school and all Girls to the Black school, was a satisfactory alternative for Ferriday.

Now that we were near completion of the 1970 school year, students such as D. Burns, our senior vice president, were sent to meet with board members concerning our class's graduation. Within his presentation, he stated that all Black students requested "Ferriday High School" be printed on their diplomas, but not with the identifying distinction of boy or girl. He also placed before the board five "proposals of Black seniors," one specifically not accepting anything but a consolidated graduation, or an all-boys (Black and White) graduation, and the same demand was made for girls. The five-part proposal that our vice president D. Burns presented to the board was viewed strongly. However, each proposal was pushed aside. To make a statement and distinguish us from the Whites, every diploma issued to the Black students carried a designation of either "Ferriday Boys High School" or "Ferriday Girls High School" printed at the very top. Meanwhile, the White students' diplomas only stated, "Ferriday High School."

Everything that was asked for in those proposals was ignored. Not to disrespect Mr. Burn's presentation—by all means, it was presented exceptionally well, though the timing appeared to have been intentionally delayed. There was no way any proposed plan already in effect would be reversed. All decisions had been locked in stone before the board even met. Regardless, his presentation did prove one thing to be a fact—attending school by sex or gender was not a solution. It was merely a form of desegregation presented by the school board, to please the court just long enough for a construction in progress to be completed.

While all of this was taking place, the Whites were not sitting still. A school was being built, and it was coming along swiftly. The following semester, spring of 1970, the majority of the White students did not return to Ferriday High School. A local Methodist church was provided for them to attend classes.

It didn't bother me that the majority of the White students didn't return to attend school with us. But what did bother me and for the world of it. Over all these years, I could never figure out who in Ferriday was influential, powerful, and persuasive enough to have a court *system's ruling delayed, just long enough for the construction of a new school to be completed.*

This had to be a powerful group of individuals, a higher echelon in the town of Ferriday so displeased by the merger of the Black and White students that they planned a strategy, one that would work in their favor, to resegregate themselves immediately after the final court's ruling. The Whites of Ferriday outsmarted everyone by building a new school within a single year. It was beyond amazing. They overpowered the court system, the school board, and most of all, the Blacks who initiated the movement.

The Whites of Ferriday were refusing to be a part of any desegregation plan. Whether it be by race, sex, or creed. By midterm of 1970, what was known to be the "Bulldogs" of Ferriday High School was no longer in existence. I believed it to be true, the mascot was discarded along with the majority of its White students, those who could afford to attend their "Newly Constructed School." We as Black male students along with the few Whites who could not afford the new school. Shared the entire semester with a "Mascot" that served no purpose at all, the town of Ferriday had abandoned its school's mascot and the school itself. The newly constructed school of Ferriday would carry a new name, the Huntington High "Hounds" of Ferriday, An "All White Private School." Out of all the schools in the Parish, Ferriday continued to be segregated.

As I write this story over fifty years later, nothing has changed other than their mascots. Ferriday High is still predominantly Black, just as the Whites had planned for it to be, the mascot has changed though to the All Mighty TROJANS. And their new private school, which now is a prominent charter school, to this day is still predominantly White. While the town of Ferriday carry a 90 to 10 percent ratio of Blacks to Whites. As you see, when Dr. King was assassinated, we, too, were dealing with our own racial war.

Honestly, it wasn't that I didn't care about the MLK aftermath or the history of his assassination. I did. It just wasn't a priority of mine because there were other things happening much closer to me, like a bomb being thrown into a fellow student's home. We all understood the purpose and the struggle of his fight, but at that time, we were all fighting for the same cause—our civil rights, namely the right just to be accepted as an equal in this great society. There were activists in our own town being harassed and burned by Whites who didn't give a damn about us or the color of our skin.

It was hard to understand at my age because there were only three channels on our black-and-white television sets, if you even had one, and they were regulated to go off at midnight. Our history textbooks only taught us about the success of the White people, even though their success seemed to have come mostly by the hands of poor and hardworking Black people.

Now, by the year 1968, the year of Dr. King's assassination, I'd grown into my own, and it was only then that I realized there must have been a part in this Civil Rights Movement I could play. I had turned sixteen and had begun to understand the concept of achieving goals through a symbolic protest, the practice of nonviolence.

When asked that summer if I would like to participate in a desegregation strategy to integrate our White public school, I could not believe it. The plan was to gather eighteen students willing to walk through the gymnasium doors of Ferriday High School on opening day. Dr. King had taught all of us how to be strong, so there was no other answer to give other than yes.

With that said, those years, from 1968 through 70, are considered a part of history in the town of Ferriday because of that desegregation strategy.

Back to 1977...

***

"Yes, Vincent! I've researched it to be room 306, and from what I've heard, that room is not for rent anymore. What do you think? Can we try?"

"Dang, girl, you are serious."

"Yes, Vincent! We're in Memphis. You have to take me."

"Sure, why not? We'll stop by Dyer's Burgers first. I've heard it's really good. Then to the motel. Do you have the name and street where it all happened?" That was important because I didn't care much for riding around in Memphis.

"Yes, the Lorraine Motel on Mulberry Street. Vincent, this is amazing. It's exciting. I can't wait." She was elated and about as happy as a Southern girl could be.

This was midway through 1977, and leaving the Southern part of the country always relieved me of some intense feelings, especially from being overly aggressive in my actions and suspicious of what could happen. Just the thought of going north was soothing to my soul. It was like taking a break from having to worry about what was coming next.

****

The visit to MLK's famous assassination landmark was amazing to Dearie and me. We stood at a distance and admired the site and its surroundings for some time before our departure. She was elated to see the exact spot of Reverend King's position when it all happened. It was something to cherish and lock into your memory bank forever.

****

We had only traveled for a few minutes once we left the site before realizing we needed gas. I pulled into a small station outside of town.

"Dearie, take this," I said, handing her a hundred-dollar bill.

"Go inside and pay for the gas? I doubt if that damn attendant sitting in front of the soda machine has any intention of serving us."

She went inside, and I secured the trigger in the lock position to pump the gas automatically. As I took a moment to clean the windshield, I saw the fellow move from the soda machine to the back of the building. He must have assumed I was trying to steal the damn gas and had sent Dearie inside to watch for me.

After finishing my usual routine, I realized it was taking her way too long to return. After grabbing my Bible off the dash, never taking my eyes off the guy who had returned to sit in front of the soda machine, I eased toward the station's door.

I pulled it open rapidly, only to find Dearie pinned against a cash register by another gentleman who was claiming her bill was counterfeit. There was no way for her to know if that were true or not, and I didn't know how he could tell the authenticity of the bill, anyway. I had no idea if the money was counterfeit or not, though I was almost positive that it wasn't. It was one of the same hundred-dollar bills I used at Doris's Dress Shop. They were all from the same stack—the five thousand dollars in the envelope from the Senator's house.

What I did know was both were in plain view. I opened my Bible.

"Let her go!" Once he released her, I beckoned quickly, nodding my head backward. "Come. Come, Dearie."

With the Bible now open and my hand resting directly on my pistol, I waited while she stumbled to get closer, and once she was close enough, I whispered, "Walk slowly to the car, and once you're inside, crank it, leaving the driver side door open."

With the nose of a Beretta 92 pointed upward at the gentleman while still lying inside the Bible, I spoke convincingly. "Come! I need you to sit next to your friend in front of this soda machine."

From the vibe I had previously gotten from him, it was obvious they were up to something. We were in a small town outside of Memphis, all alone, and what he had done to her had me furious.

Taking a chance that they would not take things further was not part of my thought process. Now, with both sitting where I could see them, it was time for us to leave.

I made it to the car, but before I could peel out, the manager shouted, "N****r, you didn't think I'd follow you?"

They were both approaching, and at that point, I didn't hesitate. I grabbed my other pistol from the console. "Stop. Turn back around and walk toward the building."

"If you gonna shoot me, do it right here."

"Fuck, I should! The way you got my girl shaking like she's having a damn seizure, I should blow the backside of your darn skull out."

"Sure, only a coward would shoot a man in the back." Suddenly, he made a move to turn around, but before he could do so, I shot him in the upper left shoulder. Then I turned to the other guy. "Would you like to follow us as well?"

"No! Please! Please! Don't shoot me!"

"I'm not. Just hand me your wallet and see that your friend gets to the hospital." I removed the picture ID from his wallet and told him never to say a word about this.

"Vincent, you shot him!"

"He had it coming. Look at you. You're shaking like a leaf on a tree. I need to get you to a hospital."

"No! Vincent, we'll go to jail."

"For what, Dearie? We didn't do anything."

"Shooting that guy and leaving him for dead, that's nothing to you?"

"Don't worry about him. I only shot him with a damn tranquilizer. In a couple of hours, he'll be fine. You, on the other hand, seem to be doing worse. You're the one in need of a doctor."

"A tranquilizer? Vincent, the guy isn't dead?"

"No, it was only a tranquilizer pistol I pulled from the console. You can relax. He'll be okay."

Dearie sighed a breath of relief. After that little tragedy, we finally made it to Interstate 40, the main highway. I could tell it was only prayer, mainly from Dearie, that kept us from being pulled over, although there was no way the attendant could tell which way we were headed, and with a slight head start, we had an advantage.

Shit!!! I never knew the potency of the chemical used in the syringe, and all I could do was hope that Franco had it right. He was someone I had faith in. He'd told me earlier, if there ever was a time your intent was not to kill, the tranquilizer gun was the one to use, and hell—my intent was never to harm him. Not only that, but I had proof—a little under five thousand dollars in my possession, and none of it I believed to be counterfeit. There was no reason for his accusation of Dearie passing off a phony bill. He was trying to threaten us out of a hundred dollars, a scam that turned bad and backfired.

We put several hundred miles behind us, still thinking we would soon be pulled over. But it never happened, and we continued our trip to Michigan without further complications.

"Flint here I come!"

To be continued.

About the Author

Noel Dias was born in Ferriday, Louisiana. After serving five years in the US Armed Forces, he embarked on training in a wide range of vocational pursuits, including electronics repair, office administration, private investigations, modeling, refrigeration and heating, and truck driving, his current field of employment. As a trucker, he has logged over 1.4 million miles of service and was awarded a specially designed 18-wheeler truck and trailer after a 17-year stint with a former employer. He has also tried his hand as an inventor, having patented the Kwick Hitch, a one-piece trailer hitch guideplate. As a fan of sports and always the competitor, Dias has participated in basketball, track, and, to this day, drag racing. Though he considers education vital to a life well lived, Dias believes the true mark of success is found in the journey, not the heights to which one climbs. Smooth: Tales of a Non-Convicted Criminal, Part II is his second book.